# Reweaving the Urban Fabric:
## Approaches to Infill Housing

Essays by
Ghislaine Hermanuz
Marta Gutman
Richard Plunz

Introduction by
Peter Marcuse

New York State Council on the Arts
Princeton Architectural Press

Deborah Norden, *Editor* NYSCA
Stewart Johnson, *Copy Editor*
Mary Lee Thompson, *Copy Editor*
Abigail Sturges, *Designer*

Library of Congress
Cataloging-in-Publication Data

Hermanuz, Ghislaine.
Reweaving the urban fabric.

Bibliography: p.
Includes index.
1. Infill housing.  2. Building sites.
3. Housing policy.  4. Land use,
Urban.  I. Gutman, Marta.  II. Plunz,
Richard.  III. Title.
HD7287.5.H37  1988  307.3′36
88-32945

Cover drawing
Jeremy Dixon, Dudgeons Wharf

Published by
**The New York State Council
on the Arts**
915 Broadway
New York, New York 10010

The New York State Council on the
Arts, (NYSCA) was formed in 1960 to
promote the arts across New York
State. The Architecture, Planning and
Design Program, one of NYSCA's four-
teen discipline areas, makes awards
and offers technical assistance in the
fields of architecture, architectural history, preservation, industrial design,
landscape architecture, urban design,
as well as urban and rural planning.
The Architecture Program grants
approximately $1.5 million each year
to organizations and individuals in its
field.

Distributed by
**Princeton Architectural Press**
37 East 7th Street
New York, New York 10003

Princeton Architectural Press pub-
lishes books of merit for people interested in archiecture and design. Its
authors stand among the most influential theorists, historians, and practitioners working today.

The books follow a tradition of fine
bookmaking. All titles are sewn, including paperbacks, so that the pages will
not fall out, all are printed on acid-free
paper and will not yellow.

Proceeds benefit
**The New York Landmarks
Conservancy**
141 Fifth Avenue
New York, New York 10010

The New York Landmarks Conservancy is dedicated to the protection,
preservation, and adaptive re-use of
architecturally and historically significant buildings. The City Ventures
Fund, which will receive proceeds from
this book, is designed to help low-to-
moderate income residents of historic
neighborhoods share directly in the
benefits of preservation without fear of
being displaced as a result of historic
rehabilitation in their community.

# Contents

## Acknowledgments
*Deborah Norden*

*William Rawn*
*Andrew Square*

This book is dedicated to the unsung heroes — those design professionals and citizens who are fighting the odds to create decent and affordable housing for our cities. There are hopeful signs, as we at the New York State Council on the Arts and the New York Landmarks Conservancy were reminded by our exhibition and symposium, but the day when our housing problems are solved is not yet here.

In the meantime, we have many people to thank for their contribution to "Reweaving The Urban Fabric." Michael Bierut for his invaluable design input; Karen Johnson for her thorough and enthusiastic research; Lisa Kahane for her "re-photography"; Pablo Vengochea and Isabel Hill for their "city view"; Robin Auchincloss and her tireless team of Columbia University architecture students for their meticulous preparation of site plans; the support staff at the New York State Council on the Arts, particularly Edna Garfinkle and Jose Hernandez, for graciously participating in this extra-curricular activity; and, finally, the visiting panelists for the Architecture, Planning and Design Program at NYSCA, who have, over several years, demonstrated through their unprecedented support of projects such as this, that the design of affordable housing is of paramount importance.

SITE A

SITE B

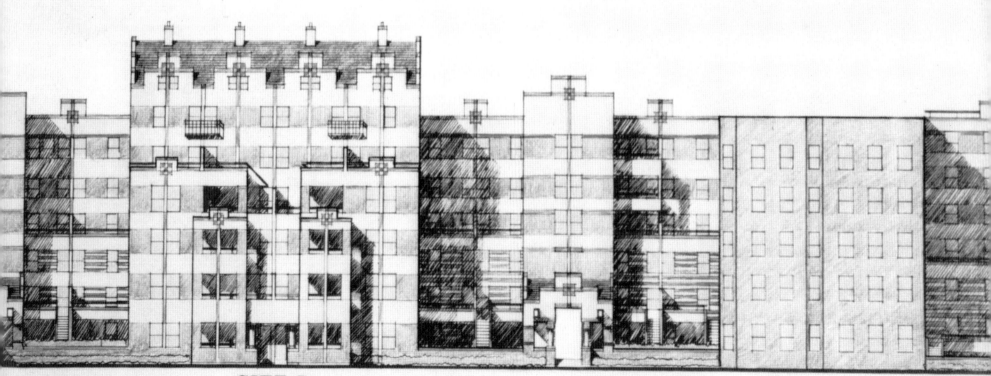

SITE B

*Michael Pyatok, Ira Oaklander, and William Vitto*
*First Place: Inner-City Infill Competition*

**Preface**
*Deborah Norden*

The Architecture, Planning and Design Program (APD) of the New York State Council on the Arts expressed concern that affordable housing had become a neglected area of current architectural practice. The program developed a national design competition for infill housing in Harlem. The goals were two-fold: to achieve excellence in the design of new and rehabilitated housing, and to meet the changing social needs of the existing inner-city community. To date, NYSCA has contributed over $150,000, the maximum available, to these efforts.

From the beginning, APD worked closely with the Harlem Urban Development Corporation; NYC Department of Housing Preservation and Development; Manhattan Community Board #10 Housing Committee; The New York Landmark's Conservancy and the West Harlem Community Organization. As the detailed program complied with city regulations and the confines of an actual site, it is possible that one or more of the winning schemes will be built.

At this time, APD would like to broaden public discussion of housing issues. Through last year's exhibition and symposium at the PaineWebber Gallery in Manhattan on the subject, some possibilities and many questions have emerged.

The challenge of designing quality affordable housing for the inhabitants of our cities has proven to be a difficult one. We need to create buildings at once socially and aesthetically appropriate. This publication addresses housing that has been designed to fill in—infill—vacant lots or blocks.

The infill approach, which integrates small sites with the existing urban fabric, has encouraged excellence in contextual design; the participation of communities in their own rehabilitation; and recognition of the city's complex history.

Many of the strongest examples of infill housing can be found in foreign cities, where governments and the architectural profession traditionally support residential construction to a degree unknown in the United States. Promising ideas can also be seen in the unbuilt projects stemming from discussions among the practitioners, students and citizens concerned about housing in American cities. We have therefore included foreign and theoretical projects in our publication. Also included here are selected projects and site plans from the PaineWebber exhibition and notes from the symposium held in conjunction with the installation. A resource bibliography will hopefully encourage others to continue research on this subject.

It is our firm belief that quality housing need not be "luxury" housing and that communities across the country can be encouraged to be involved in the creation of better and more affordable housing.

*James Harb and Elliott Rosenblum*
*Manhattan Valley Townhouses*

Bad housing is one of the scandals of our society; no housing at all—homelessness—is perhaps our society's most visible shame today. Hundreds of thousands of residents of the United States, the richest country in the history of the world, are sleeping on the streets and in shelters where conditions rival the worst of mediaeval shelter. In some railroad stations the floors are washed with lye to discourage the hundreds who otherwise sleep in cardboard boxes in the passageways. Police are used to force people into shelters they consider so noxious they would rather sleep outside building entrances in the coldest nights than go to them. Hundreds of thousands of people in the nation's largest city are living with rats, broken windows, leaking roofs, dangerous hallways, without heat or hot water. Transportation facilities are classified as "group quarters" by the Bureau of the Census because they have so many regular residents. In the face of all of this, the Federal government has called a halt to all construction of additional housing for the poor, and the city government in New York resists providing adequate shelter for the poor because "they might want to stay there permanently," yet gives tax abatements for million-dollar condominiums and sees the promotion of more luxury housing as a desirable city objective. "Scandal" and "shame" are words too mild for these conditions.

This volume has a direct relevance to the melange of cruelty, neglect, and sybaritism that housing in the U.S. has become. Professionals in the design fields—architects and planners—can play a role in changing things. Not a decisive role, perhaps, but a significant one. We can refuse to do wrong (Hippocrates' "*primum non nocere*" isn't a bad rule for us also): refuse to build barracks for the homeless, or demolish historic structures, or build to inhumane standards, or despoil the environment. We can criticize, loudly and publicly, the conditions and the individuals that make it impossible for us to do the work we were—we hope—trained to do, to build in a humane and life-respecting fashion. Such criticism is sometimes the only thing we can do, for the opportunities to build decent housing for those most in need are not plentiful today, and the conditions that create those opportunities are not within the control of professionals.

All the more important, therefore, that planning professionals working in the built environment support the creation of such opportunities as fully as they can and use them wisely when they appear. The 1985 Inner City Infill housing competition, sponsored by the New York State Council on the Arts, was one such opportunity and the contributors to this volume are in the best traditions of their respective professions. Infill housing, as it was conceived, is the opposite of "slum clearance" and displacement. It represents integration of buildings—and their residents—into the existing social fabric, not their separation and exclusion. It represents respect for existing life styles and social patterns, rather than arrogant and elitist efforts to "reform" the poor and benighted. Given the present political context, in which the isolation and neglect of the poor, of minority group members, of household patterns not conforming to the conservative mainstream, are the watchwords, infill housing is a slogan of resistance and progress.

We should not, however, delude ourselves about how great an influence good infill housing models can have. Certainly bad design contributed to the bad name public housing now has in some circles, by creating high-rise boxes in which families were warehoused. But low quality high-rise public housing is a product of a hostile real estate industry, an uncommitted Congress, and a cowardly bureaucracy much more than of a failure of imagination by design professionals. Good high-rises and good public housing are within the tradition of socially responsive architecture. Architects and planners should have been much more outspoken in demanding higher standards and better funding for publicly-oriented housing programs. But we could not change things by ourselves then, and we cannot do so now. Designing good, context-sensitive infill housing rather than isolated unwelcome projects that intrude in the urban landscape is a real contribution to better housing and better cities. To imagine that it is enough to show the way, and all will follow, however, is a dangerous delusion. The underlying causes of bad housing, which go far beyond the lack of imagination or social responsibility of the professions, must also be addressed. None the less, we have not covered ourselves with glory in the field over the last forty years. Both the design of bad public housing, and the design of (good or bad) luxury housing without consideration of its social impacts, aggravate some of the most serious problems of our society. A few have always fought for improvements in housing for the poor; it is time that organized professionals get into the fray as well, and go public with some strong statements about the most critical problem confronting their professions.

Infill housing deals with a particularly important part of that problem today. The tensions between rebuilding the old and starting anew, and between infill housing and "green fields" construction, is an old one. In the 1920s the best of professional opinion was on the side of new development, and not without good arguments. In a period of rapid growth, garden cities have an attraction infill housing cannot match. But today, in a period of population stability and often decline, and of political and social and racial reaction, the situation is reversed. The realities of past abandonment and present stagnation make infill today the cutting edge of progress.

This book, and the exhibition that preceded it, are therefore heartily to be welcomed. They reflect an increasing awareness both of what needs to be done and what can be done to provide decent housing. They help restore the social content inextricably linked to the aesthetic work of architects, designers, and planners. The goal of the program suggested for participants are models of what should be required of all housing: attention to public and semi-public as well as private spaces, integration of services and community facilities with housing, scale suited to neighborhood, attention to aesthetics and peoples' perceptions of their environment, and unit configuration reflecting diversity of users and needs. The steps from design to actuality are giant steps indeed, and it is no surprise that so few of these proposals are in imminent danger of being built. But they help dispel the notion that "we" do not know how to design good housing; they provide, graphically and in articulate fashion, good models for some of what needs to be done. The next step is to get it done.

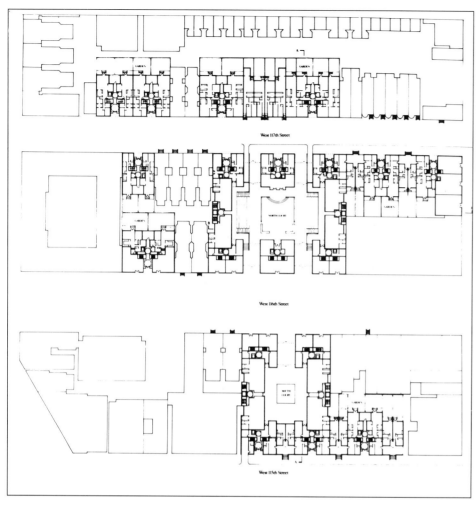

West 117th Street

West 116th Street

West 115th Street

*Marta Gutman, Eugene Sparling, Ann Kalla, Richard Plunz, John Ambrose, Blake Auchincloss, Ellen Belknapp, Martine Kornier, Ellen Kuhn, Jylle Menoff, and Maurizid De Vita*
*Entry: Inner-City Infill Competition*

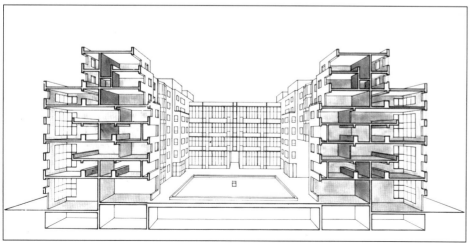

INNER-CITY

CITY

INFILL

## Infill Housing: A Remedy to Harlem's Deterioration

*Ghislaine Hermanuz*

*Michael Bierut*
*Poster: Inner-City Infill Competition*

For the people of Harlem, housing is one of the most important issues of community development. By now, most of the older stock—up to 70% of the properties in Central Harlem—has been abandoned. [Illus. 1] If in the 1960's, the best way to resolve the housing crisis was seen as Urban Renewal and its massive relocation of people from substandard tenements into newer, therefore assumed to be better, public housing projects, it soon became apparent that the projects' occupants felt alienated by the new places whose development had required gutting existing neighborhoods and destroying the social and economic bonds, however fragile, which made them viable. During the 1970's, therefore, planners began to substitute rehabilitation and preservation of the older housing stock for Urban Renewal, believing this approach less detrimental to the existing social fabric of the community. But they failed to take into account the fact that the majority of the buildings they sought to recycle had been rejected decades ago as prototypes because of the poor environmental qualities such buildings engendered. Uncoordinated rehabilitation of basically substandard housing stock cannot alone revitalize a neighborhood. Thus the debate of the 1980's centers on parallel concerns of housing quantity and quality, questions of affordability, and, most importantly, the role housing development can play in a community fighting to regain its economic, its cultural, and its political identity.

Today, in terms of housing for Harlem, the two pressing issues remain availability and affordability. Housing activists are currently discussing new approaches to housing development which will ensure that, over time, dwellings will remain available to low and moderate-income people. Among the principles of development that these activists consider, community land trusts and mutual housing associations appear most realistic. A community land trust, a non-profit corporation designed to own land and hold it in trust for a collective, can protect land from market fluctuations and speculation and makes it possible to direct public subsidies to the development of housing for the poor. Because such housing will not be merely a socially acceptable way of making money in the non-profit development sector, it stands a better chance of becoming a permanent resource of stable homes for the poor. Mutual housing associations, equally non-profit, can then administer these subsidies.

Until now, little research has been done to test design responses to these development models and the affordable housing they are to generate. In this respect, the challenge to designers and architectural students responding to the *Inner City Infill: Housing for Harlem* competition, proposed in 1985 by the New York State Council on the Arts, was precisely to design a prototypical solution for socially responsive housing, affordable to the poor, which would insert itself into the gaps left in Harlem's urban fabric by the selective demolition caused by Urban Renewal and, later, by abandonment.

1
*Townhouse street.*

Opportunities for design innovations today stem from drastic changes in the context of housing production. For one thing, the climate for housing development has changed. There are no longer the ready-made government funding programs that once shaped design strategies. In the absence of federal monies, new resources have to be sought. Inevitably, a larger role will now be given the private sector, whose development objectives are most often incompatible with the creation of affordable housing. The extent to which privately controlled development will determine who will live in Harlem is a much debated political issue. Fear of gentrification is a reality. For the architect committed to low-income housing, the question remains: can a funding strategy be derived from or generated by a design concept? In addition to decline of traditional financing, users' needs have changed. Today, whether new or rehabilitated, housing has to meet the needs of smaller families, single-parent households, and families with two working adults. Such housing must be suitable for unrelated adults sharing accommodations and for elderly and younger people cohabiting within the same space. Plans for new housing must address the need for shelter of the homeless, too, and of families that are now doubled-up when not tripled-up in the small apartments of housing projects. The social structure of a black community, its economic needs, and the realities of its daily life are both specific and diverse enough to constitute a profound challenge to the design standards which are prevalent in the minds of middle-class architects designing for low and moderate income clients.

Housing in Harlem today must be seen as only one aspect of an overall community economic revitalization process. The residential space must be able to accommodate self-generated economic activities in a society structurally unable to provide enough jobs for its socially, economically, and politically disfranchised population. Rethinking, for instance, the delivery of social services in increments small enough to be integrated into housing patterns is one option. New health clinics, senior citizens advisory services, child care, after-school and skills-development programs are activities that can enhance a residential development by offering quality services as an extension of the private residential space. In addition, the dwelling unit itself can be transformed so that the private residential space houses money-making activities: a well designed kitchen can allow a cook to cater lunches for neighborhood workers; in a properly zoned living room, a computer can generate a word-processing business; a flexible room can become a dressmaker's workshop or turn into a small child-care unit. Transforming private residential spaces to accommodate income generators is a step toward more self-reliant communities. The very process of building housing must be designed so that it too can become a permanent source of job opportunities, from construction to maintenance. Housing can be designed around a system of prefabricated, locally made elements. Apartments can be outfitted with building parts, furniture, and finishing, produced by a community-controlled construction industry.

Neglect, aborted Urban Renewal activities, and continued abandonment have created a physical reality that necessitates the rehabilitation of those structures which can still be salvaged and, on relatively small sites, bold interventions with new construction, designed to fill in the voids that currently scar the urban fabric of Harlem. Specific parameters of an acceptable approach to rehabilitation have to be set in order to avoid the disastrously inadequate responses of the 1970's. Such guidelines have to ensure the possibility of transforming the present socio-physical structure of the block and creating, through a combination of rehabilitation and new construction, a different spatial order. Thus, rehabilitation can be part of an overall transformation rather than a mere refurbishing of what already exists. The dilemma posed by rehabilitation in Harlem is not just the choice between rebuilding a past that was once ruled out as unfit for human needs or replacing it by a brand new housing type. More importantly, it implies a choice between reinforcing the expression of class structure in the physcial environment, by relegating the poor once again to refurbished tenements, while the new housing is slated for the better-offs, or inventing a new physical order to represent a more equitable distribution of space according to needs rather than ability to consume.

No less important for the designer's mandate is the political pressure of a community for whom gentrification is not just an economic threat but also a cultural one. For Harlem to remain the cultural focal point of Afro-America, displacement of its present occupants must be stopped, together with land-use patterns and housing financing practices which, by allowing only 20% of new housing to be subsidized, discriminate in favor of the well-to-do. Since racism still prevents Blacks and Hispanics from free access to much alternative housing, maintaining Harlem for them is a cultural necessity. When Harlem gains control over its land-use decisions through land ownership, whether individual or collective, through cooperatives or mutual housing associations, self-determination will be achieved. These new forms of ownership and tenure will have a radical impact on architectural design. Infill housing is perhaps the best opportunity for creating a housing type capable of responding to all these pressures, which, for the designer, translate into two sets of design objectives. The first set defines specific guidelines to ensure the viability of Harlem as a socio-physical context. The second suggests direction for responding to the changing structures of low-income, urban households and the real cultural needs of an Afro-American community, thus promoting new concepts of livability.

The Inner City Infill Housing competition organized by the New York State Council on the Arts in 1985, sought to respect the qualities of the physical context of Harlem as a residential neighborhood. Low-scale developments; wide avenues; 19th Century limestone and brownstone townhouses displaying wide variations of architectural details; tenements, both Old Law and New Law, traditionally housing the working class; and the turn-of-the-century elevator buildings along major avenues, today compose the Harlem landscape and define its quality as a place of residence. In contrast, high-rise public housing projects of the 1950's and 1960's do not respect the definition of the block by providing a continuous street wall, nor do they display the decorative cornices, rooflines, window casements, and door frames, or the entry porches and stoops of contrasting materials, which adorn older houses and lend identity to each individual structure, while adding richness and continuity to the streetscape. With contextualism, rehabilitation of existing buildings and new construction must be seen as one integrated intervention, generating a series of new, contemporary, prototypical buildings.

Reinforcing the quality of the historical urban landscape is a necessary but not sufficient improvement. If early twentieth-century tenements offer well designed, carefully executed classical facades, they also mask substandard, poorly lit and ventilated residential spaces within the very same spaces that today's renovation

2
*Streetscape with people.*

plans for Harlem reserved for the working classes since, as they are seen as symbols of oppression, these renovated living spaces are not attractive to the well-to-do. Yet, it is possible to infuse new life into these tenements, preserving their most valuable assets, their public facades, while gutting the interiors, and obliterating their original footprint to make their programmatic transformations possible.

The livability of the neighborhood, after its reconstruction, can be measured by the way it promotes social interaction, gives people a sense of community and security, and enables them to control their physical, economic and social environment. Programming and designing of public areas, the addition of services and economic functions to reactivate the residential spaces proper, and the creative use of open spaces, all these can generate new building configurations. Producing a more flexible environment begins with an analysis of the private dwelling and of the building's shared spaces to determine which space standards need upgrading, within a redistribution of individual and collective domains. [Illus. 2]

Architects who competed in the *Inner City Infill: Housing for Harlem* competition and students working on the same brief responded with proposals for building prototypes that ranged from a contemporary interpretation of the townhouses and tenements of earlier days to new models of low-rise, high-density structures. Whether separate from or inclusive of rehabilitation, some of these building concepts were radically new for the area. The prototypes had to be replicable, yet flexible enough to fit a variety of site conditions. They had to provide alternatives to traditional apartments to suit households other than the nuclear family; and they had to explore the potential for various design strategies to redefine the spatial relationships between the private and public realms of housing. Finally, they had to be affordable.

The competition program itself called for 420 units of new and rehabilitated housing, with an additional 33,000 square feet of commercial space and 7,000 square feet of space earmarked for community services and facilities. On-site parking was limited to 80 cars, well below what the current zoning code mandates. Apartment sizes represented minimal standards commonly used today and were to be guidelines only. Development of an economical construction system was recommended with, for the competition first-stage winners only, the added requirements of a cost-analysis of their final scheme. Perhaps paradoxically, the program demanded that competitors meet zoning, space standards, and building code requirements of New York City, while still pursuing innovative solutions that, inevitably, must challenge some if not all of these very rules.

The development parcels forming the site are located in Central Harlem, in the blocks from West 115th Street to West 118th Street, between Lenox Avenue to the East, and Adam Clayton Powell Jr. Boulevard to the West. The site, made up of city-owned properties, contains a mix of vacant lots, abandoned buildings, and inhabited structures. Some of the more dilapidated tenements are slated for demolition. The empty lots are not necessarily contiguous, and new construction would

4

Main map labels:

Subway Stop  125th  Subway Stop

Historic District

St. Martins Church  Watchtower

Marcus Garvey Park

Amsterdam Ave

Morningside Drive

Morningside Ave

Manhatten Ave

Frederick Douglass Blvd.

St Nicholas Ave

Adam Clayton Powell Blvd.

Lenox Ave

5th Ave

Madison Ave

Park Ave

Competition Site

P.S. 149

Graham Court

Subway Stop  116th  Subway Stop

115th St. Branch N.Y. Public Library

Martin Luther King Houses

Playground

Taft Houses

110th

Central Park

☐ Historic Landmark

0  200  400  750
100  300  500

North

5
*Graham Court.*

6
*The Mosque.*

7
*117th Street.*

5

6

7

have to be fitted between existing structures, some of which would be renovated in conjunction with the new development. With the exception of 116th Street and Lenox Avenue, both of which have ground-floor commercial frontages, the site is residential. The Mosque, at the southwest corner of Lenox Avenue and 116th Street, and the Graham Court apartment house, on Adam Clayton Powell Jr. Boulevard, between 116th and 117th Streets, are the most prominent architectural structures on the site; and lend it a recognizable identity. [Illus. 3–7]

The former richness of life in Harlem is clearly present in this neighborhood. Opposite the Graham Court is a triangular square, named after A. Philip Randolph, the black labor leader. Nearby can be found the Hotel Cecil, which once housed Minton's Playhouse, where famed jazz musicians, including Thelonius Monk and Dizzy Gillespie, created "be-bop" in late night jam sessions, in the 1940's and 50's. St. Thomas the Apostle Church still displays its fine terracotta, neo-Gothic facade. On the southwest corner of 116th Street and Adam Clayton Powell Jr. Boulevard stands the first building designed as a motion picture house in New York, the R.K.O. Regent Theater; now it is the home of one of the largest religious congregations in Harlem. Around the corner, on 115th Street, the Renaissance facade of one of McKim, Mead and White's most handsome branch libraries faces the once famous Wadsleigh High School for Girls, now a junior high school. The greenery of Central Park is just a few blocks away, and so is the bustle of 125th Street. [Illus. 8–10]

Development strategies opened to the *Inner City Infill: Housing for Harlem* competition designers reflect the urbanistic dilemmas of intervention in an inner-city context. Roughly, they fall into the following categories:

I. *Unit of development: large site vs. traditional, narrow lot*
Projects fall into two models, reflecting present day housing development practice in New York; i.e., the assemblage of sites large enough to be economically developed by the private sector, on the one hand, and the reuse of the basic twenty to twenty-five foot wide lot, singly or in the aggregate, on the other. The prototypes generated range thus from townhouses to mid-rise elevator buildings. Because the competition site is divided into parcels large enough to suggest their possible distribution to various developers, it was on a set of clearly defined design guidelines that the burden of ensuring unity and quality of the whole had to rest.

With townhouse schemes, economy stems from repetition, not from size; the trend is towards using the same prototypical townhouse throughout the project, with some small amount of variation at the level of architectural detailing, possibly selected by the users themselves or with programmatic and density variation, to reflect the specialness of a streetscape.

With larger buildings, economies of scale are achieved by servicing a sizable number of apartments with one vertical circulation core, one that offers the amenity of an elevator. Variations from one scheme to another occur at the level of the design of the shared spaces, from corridors to lobbies and pooled open spaces. [Illus. 11–13]

8
*A. Philip Randolph Square.*

9
*Regent's Theater.*

8

9

**19**

**10**
View to 125th Street.

**11**
The townhouse is not just a response to the context but a device to achieve a high-density residential space of quality. Giannoula Pavlakos. Axonometric and facade.

**12**
Moreover, a townhouse can be a means to achieve a ratio of homeowners to renters suitable for Harlem, and "houses that pay for themselves." Stephen Campbell and Mark Nielson. Facade.

**13**
Users can select some of the building features within the options offered by the construction system. Stephen Campbell and Mark Nielson. Axonometric.

10

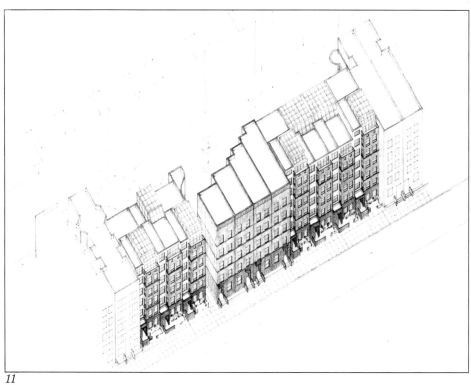

11

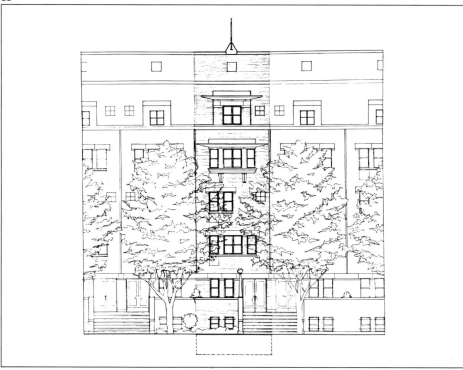

12

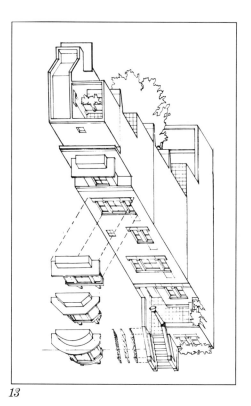

13

*14a,b*
*Distribution of housing along narrow interior mews or around multiple small courtyards tends to privatize the interior of the block. Michael Pyatok and Ira Oaklander (a).*
*Susanna Torre (b).*
*Site Plans.*

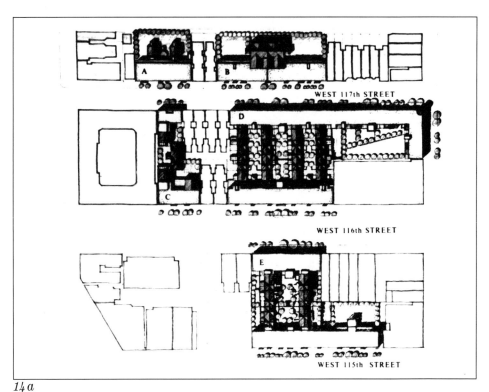

14 a

14 b

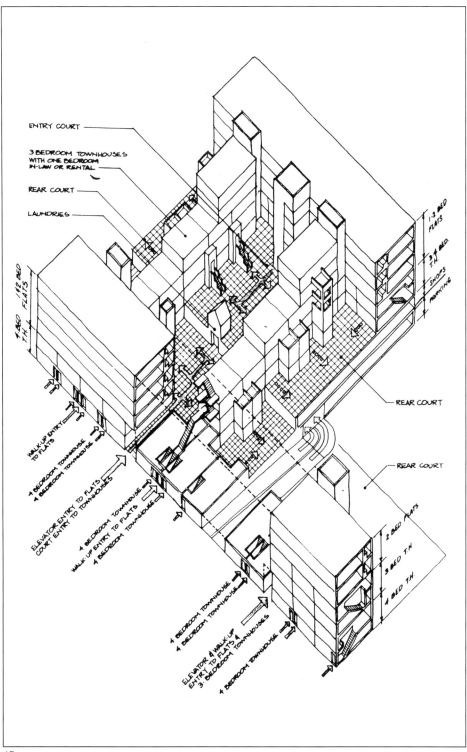

ENTRY COURT

3 BEDROOM TOWNHOUSES
WITH ONE BEDROOM
IN-LAW OR RENTAL

REAR COURT

LAUNDRIES

1-2 BED FLATS

3-4 BED T.H.

SHOPS

PARKING

1 BED / 1-2 BED FLATS
T.H.

REAR COURT

WALK-UP ENTRY TO FLATS

4 BEDROOM TOWNHOUSE
4 BEDROOM TOWNHOUSES

ELEVATOR ENTRY TO FLATS
COURT ENTRY TO TOWNHOUSES

4 BEDROOM TOWNHOUSE
WALK-UP ENTRY TO FLATS
4 BEDROOM TOWNHOUSE

REAR COURT

2 BED FLATS

3 BED T.H.

4 BED T.H.

4 BEDROOM TOWNHOUSE
4 BEDROOM TOWNHOUSE

ELEVATOR & WALK-UP
ENTRY TO FLATS &
3-BEDROOM TOWNHOUSES

4 BEDROOM TOWNHOUSE

## II. *Character of the block: privatizing the block's interior vs. increasing its public function*

Proposals organizing the dwellings off interior mews and courtyards, as well as those distributing them in a carpetlike fashion, turn the interior of the block into a very private space, whereas those that have introduced cross and through-block pedestrian or vehicular passages, often lined with commercial work, and service space, increase the quantity and quality of the public environment. The transformation of the existing grid with the addition of streets, and the shorter blocks thus produced, are ways of ensuring control of the shared public spaces as well as securing their constant maintenance by the government.

In mews schemes, penetration into the block's internal space is typically controlled by the use of gates. This provides security and defensibility at the cost of reduced accessibility to the general public. A class differentiation is implied between those whose individual *maisonettes* are entered directly from the protected mews and those whose apartments overlook and are accessible from the street.

In contrast, schemes that increase the public domain open up possibilities for collective life and enterprises. Workshops, produce greenmarkets, day-care centers, public squares: all of these amenities can be shared with the larger community and are made safe by their active use. [Illus. 14–17]

## III. *Contextualism: historical references vs. contemporary expression*

The emphasis on contextualism, which includes respect for period details and compliance with existing building heights, together with a purposefully ambiguous program that suggested rather than mandated the transformation of the dwelling unit, led many competitors to reinvent existing tenement or townhouse forms, as well as to mimic their character. The more successful projects share an ability to accommodate the old and insert new elements, without sacrificing the opportunity for a contemporary expression. Interpretations of stoops, screen walls used to maintain the continuity of the street facade, tower-like buildings rising from bases that conform to the neighborhood style and bulk, are devices used to renew the architectural expression of old prototypes. While the street facades appear to blend in the old fabric, significant changes often happen when, above the sixth floor level, completely new typologies arise; or when the internal face of the block turns into a carefully designed frontage, giving character to the block's interior semi-public spaces, rather than merely framing a left-over rear yard. [Illus. 18–24].

## IV. *Economic strategy: minimizing space standards vs. creating a new economic base*

Many of the schemes presented elaborate proposals for mixed-use neighborhoods, including spaces for formal and informal economic activities, weaving them at times into the dwellings themselves. The impact on design of new ways to finance the construction of a building and to consider its maintenance costs over time suggests the need for tenure formulas mixing individual ownership and rental. Sometimes, the residental space is conceived in such a way as to include a flexible room that can be used to generate income for the occupants or as a rental to outsiders. Other times, the dwelling space is located adjacent to or within easy access of commercial areas, and can be linked to them.

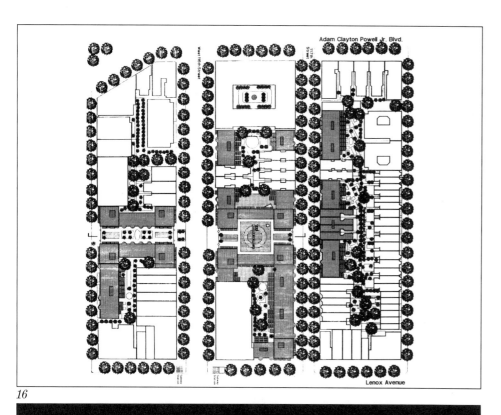

16

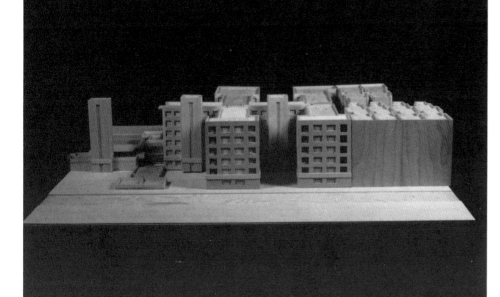

17

16
*Public spaces can be expanded by creating new through-block streets, sometimes for pedestrians only, with community services along them. Secundino Fernandez.*
*Plan.*

17
*The sidewalk space can begin to penetrate the block, articulating the buildings and increasing the publicness of the space. Christian Zapatka.*
*Plan and elevation.*

18
*Respect of the context can be interpreted
literally, although today's construction
techniques could only reproduce 19th
Century details at a prohibitive cost.
Secundino Fernandez.
Elevation.*

19
*Once continuity has been established,
typologies new for the area can be
introduced: a tower at a prominent
corner can be inserted. Kevin Dakan,
Daniel Flebut, and Jeff Kieffer.
Perspective.*

20
*The use of a contemporary
architectural vocabulary can be
appropriate when contextual with
respect to the bulk and its modulation.
Brian McGrath.
Elevation.*

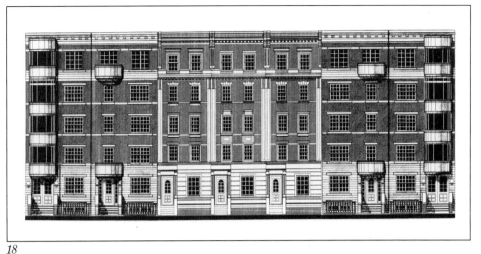

18

19

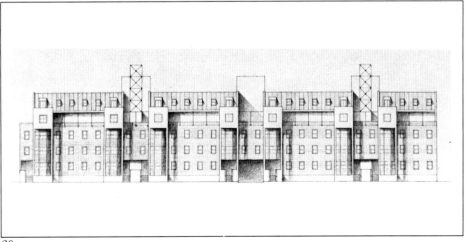

20

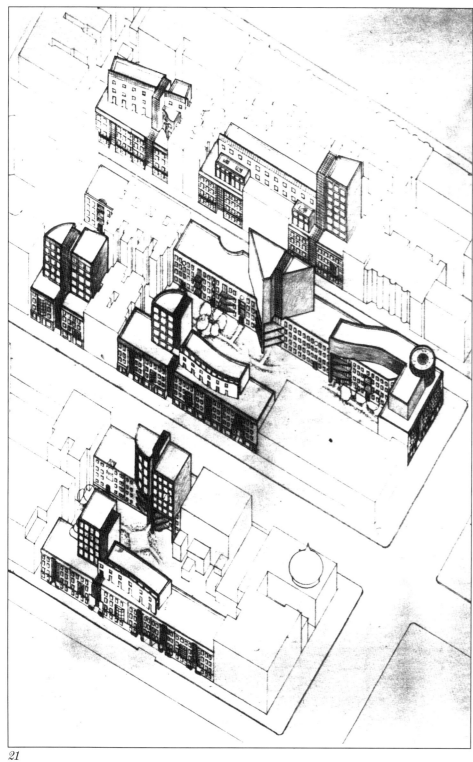

21

22

**21**
*Thus, a new city can be created atop the old one. David Bergman. Axonometric.*

**22**
*The new elements above the bulk of the traditional city can also be green recreation spaces rather than buildings. Lev Weisbach. Perspective.*

**23**
*The site ground level can be organized around a mix of economic activities: stores, market stalls, workshops, craft outlets, community services employing the local population, create an image of activity. Jill Stoner and Charles Duncan.*
*Site plan.*

**24**
*The home itself can accommodate a workplace within the dwelling's flexible spaces or as a special room for the occupant to work in or rent out. Jill Stoner and Charles Duncan.*
*Plan.*

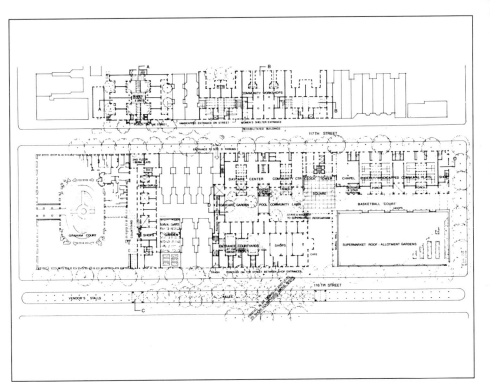

23

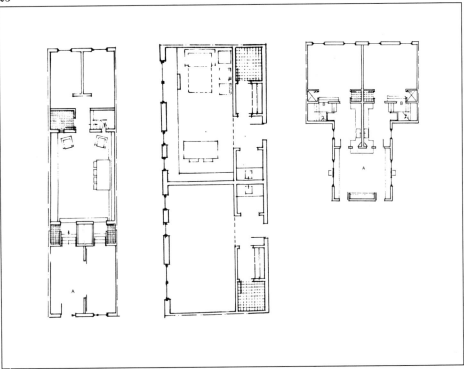

24

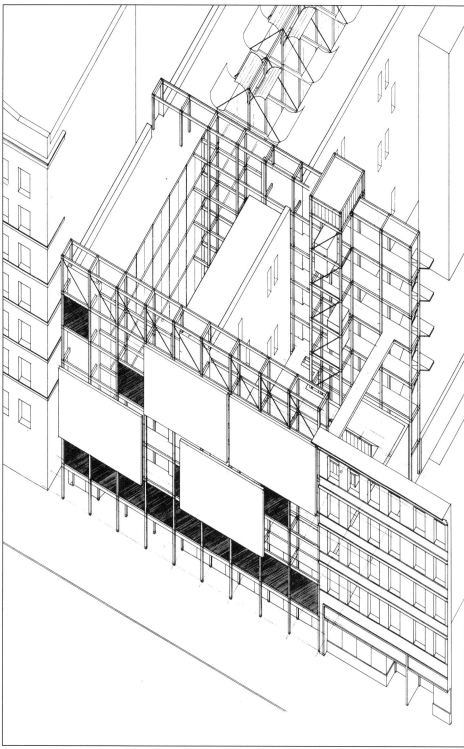

25
*A through-block, ground level arcade creates a new public path for pedestrians and the opportunity to locate commercial spaces small enough for rental to local merchants as a mini-market. Sergei Bischak. Axonometric.*

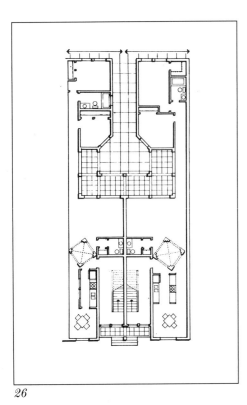

26

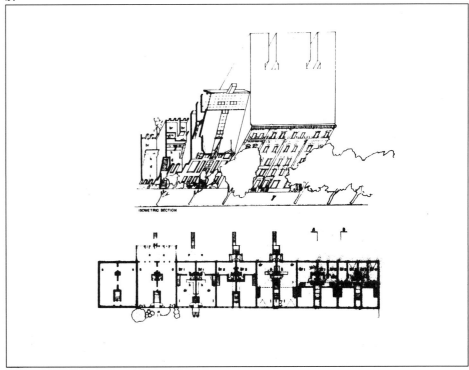

6ᵀᴴ FLOOR PLAN

GROUND FLOOR PLAN

3ᴿᴰ 5ᵀᴴ FLOOR PLAN

BASEMENT PLAN

2ᴺᴰ 4ᵀᴴ FLOOR PLAN

27

ISOMETRIC SECTION

28

Minimizing spaces often leads to traditional building forms for example, double-loaded corridor slab buildings, where the main circulation is horizontal; or new versions of the tenement, where the organizing circulation is vertical and concentrated in one place. Neither of these solutions is really satisfactory, however. Because of today's zoning requirements for light and air, double-loaded corridor slabs, on 100-foot deep lots, become very thin indeed and fail to allow for adequate room depths, while the updated *"tenements"* establish a ratio of circulation to habitable area the precludes spaciousness. [Illus. 23–25]

## V. *Rehabilitation: creating a new spatial order vs. repeating the past*
Infill can do more than put up a new building where one is now missing. Potentially, it can transform the spatial order of a partially developed block, creating a hierarchy of spaces different from that inherited from nineteenth-century development patterns. The degree to which buildings to be rehabilitated participate in this new order, how they are transformed, or how in turn they generate new forms, are the keys to the success of the new places thus produced.

Proposals that use juxtaposable townhouses as basic modules can accommodate existing structures without having them undergo major transformations, since the new townhouses are designed, as were the old ones, on similar principles of vertical circulation. Changes to existing tenements might perhaps include a reduction of their depth, allowing a more generous rear yard, or the addition of one or two floors of living spaces, making the introduction of an elevator to the vertical circulation system more economical.

In most cases, however, the changes are more substantial than these. Linkage of existing tenements to the horizontal corridor system of new buildings can make possible a greater variety of apartment layouts, although such a strategy must recognize that the floor-to-ceiling heights of the old tenements is no longer economical for modern construction. The more extreme approaches have used remaining groups of tenements as buffer zones between pockets of redeveloped spaces, considering the existing structures as shells to be filled with new uses. In some cases, the facade is the only element retained, as a screen wall which expresses, on the street side, continuity with the past, and, on its internal face, protection for the new house. [Illus. 26–27]

## VI. *Socio-cultural strategy: low-income housing vs. urban housing for Harlem*
Perhaps the most intriguing analysis of the projects is one which tries to identify design features expressive of Harlem's specificity as a black community, beyond the ubiquitous stoops and the stereotypical basket-ball courts. Dwelling units capable of housing intergenerational family groups; single young adults sharing larger accommodations; allowances for economic activities, from child care to catering; the designation of open spaces for activities such as street vending and market-style commerce, mixing rather than segregating the different age groups and economic groups; collective rather than individual control of the semi-public spaces; institutional spaces closely knitted into the residential fabric: these are themes of black culture that could have been elaborated on more in the designs submitted to the *Inner City Infill: Housing for Harlem* competition. It is significant that those proposals most responsive to a collective or communal life style come closer to expressing the urban character of the site, while the others seem to recreate the isolation and alienation of suburbia. [Illus. 28–31]

26
*The tenement does not need to be changed for its spaces to be transformed: a clever design of the lightless interior can give it a new life, if not spaciousness. John Christenson. Plan.*

27
*Cutting down the tenements' depth and designing the new apartments along a horizontal corridor, tying the old to the new, generates a new prototypical structure. Oral Selkridge.*

28
*Dwelling units themselves or "found spaces" within the overall development, can be designed for special user-groups: single parents, the homeless, young adults sharing, etc. Troy West and Anker West. Section.*

29
*Statement. Armistead Reeds.*

30
*A building parts factory can be part of
the site development and offer jobs to
the population as well as the elements
they need to suit their dwellings to their
needs. Jonathan Friedman and Judith
Sheine*
*Axonometric.*

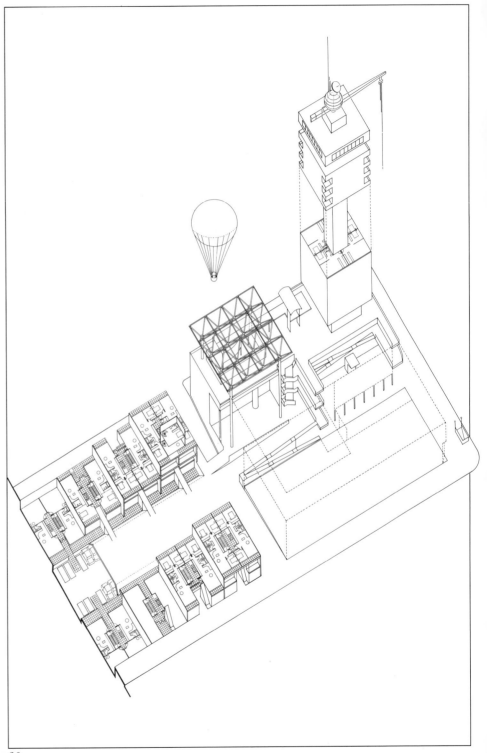

30

I  Window Well Interior from 3rd floor

II  Backyards from 3rd floor

A  Residential Street

B  View from Typical Porch

III  Mews Entrance

IV  Child's View of Mews

C  Across Upper Level Terraces - 4th floor

D  Backyards

31

*By imagining the various aspects of the occupants' lives, a very fine-tuned, responsible programming of the collective and semi-private spaces can be designed. Stephen Campbell and Mark Nielson.*
*Series of sketches.*

Note:
Some of the ideas discussed in this essay are further elaborated in books such as Shadrach Woods, *The Man in the Street: A Polemic on Urbanism* (New York, 1975), *The Community Land Trust Handbook* (Emmaus, PA), The Columbia University Community Design Workshop, *A Housing Platform for Harlem* (New York, 1985) and the New York State Council on the Arts, *Inner City Infill: A Housing Competition for Harlem* (New York, 1985). The latter provides information on the competition context and program.

The most exciting problem raised by the competition, and perhaps a challenge that only few were willing to meet, was the determination of culture-specific elements that would begin to identify the project unmistakably as "housing for Harlem." Since the 1960's, Jane Jacobs' views of city-making have become the paradigm of good residential neighborhoods for the poor. Her image of friendly neighborhoods, multi-functional and diverse, their streets made safe by the watchful eyes of civic-minded citizens, may have been seminal in its day, as such a concept pointed out the limitations of the Garden City of Ebenezer Howard and the Radiant City of Le Corbusier. Jacob's ideal of community life continues to influence current principles of housing design and few architects have taken the time to challenge it. Although it may still have some validity for small towns, such an ideal is not relevant to today's life in an inner-city black community. How often can black mothers afford to stay at home, watching from kitchen windows their children at play on a sidewalk or in a backyard? Most likely, they are working or seeking employment and the children are, if lucky, in some day-care center; the children may be the ones preparing dinner for their working mothers, yet nothing in the way designers conceive of kitchens reflect that eventuality.

Architecture has done very little to validate black people's daily lives and, therefore, the way they must use their individual or collective space. Privatizing the interior of a residential block and restricting it to luxury housing, or designing inflexible apartments, not only creates a class structure but petrifies it in the physical environment. It consolidates fears of gentrification which, in the case of Harlem, can have profound cultural implications: gentrification threatens not just the economic composition of the neighborhood, but its racial composition, too. The issue, then, is one of finding a redevelopment scale and a program that will insure that affordable units are generated, and that they are designed with consideration for their present users and their needs, whether those users are stable, gainfully employed citizens, or people marginally incorporated in the economy, or even, in some cases, temporarily homeless and jobless, and that such housing can be community sponsored, controlled, and maintained.

Arguably, the need of Harlem residents for urban housing will not be met by suburban dreams of *"ticky-tacky boxes,"* as recently seen in the South Bronx, on Charlotte Street, or in East Brooklyn, with the Niemiah development. Nor will it be met by another rendition of social Darwinism, with its illusions of well-being and its luxury towers and shanties, sorting out the rich from the poor. The need is clearly for an architectural sensibility which affirms the struggle for dignity and full citizenship of the Harlem community. It is to the credit of many of the projects submitted to the *Inner City Infill* competition that their authors were willing to tackle at least some aspects of this relevant social issue in an architecturally innovative, yet practical way.

Our present view, dictated by the economics of the real estate market, that only the rich can live in urban centers, needs to be challenged relentlessly. Thus, the ideas that infill housing development has begun to raise should be refined and pursued. The flexibility of infill and its potential to create affordable housing for the poor and revitalize inner-city neighborhoods will be fully tested when, in the near future, construction of infill developments begins to take place all over Harlem.

## Housed Together:
## The Shape of Urban Infill
*Marta Gutman*

*We must content ourselves with arranging bits of contemporary architecture within old tissues that are in more or less good condition but often completely destructured.*[1]

*Herman Hertzberger*
*Haarlemmer Houtuinen*

New York City faces an enormous housing crisis. Sixty thousand people are estimated homeless while the vacancy rate of private rental housing has dropped to less than three per cent. Public housing offers little hope for alternative shelter with the New York City Housing Authority's waiting list consisting of over 165,000 families. To satisfy this need alone the Authority needs to double the 174,000 units it now either owns or manages. Yet the construction of publicly funded housing has dropped to a mere trickle. The federal budget cuts of the 1970s and 1980s, culminating in the Reagan administration's dismantling of the nation's public housing program, have removed federal subsidies for the construction of public housing in New York City and elsewhere in the United States. Though private groups have tried to fill the housing gaps, especially by providing emergency and transitional shelters for the homeless, the city desperately needs affordable housing for its low- and moderate-income residents.[2]

The "Inner City Infill Competition," sponsored by the New York State Council on the Arts in 1985, recognized New York City's need for affordable housing and argued that its construction should be tied to the tradition of urban infill.[3] In recent years the city fabric made by party-wall building has provided a powerful alternative to that created by the urban transformations of the post-war era.[4] Its continuous yet varied urban form, produced through a process often labeled "infill building," contrasts with that produced by the insertion of free-standing towers and slabs into spaces created by slum clearance (Illus. l).[5] In infill building new construction slips into available space in the existing city, often using historically evolved low-rise, high-density housing types such as the row house and perimeter block. Greeting rather than confronting the fabric, these buildings re-establish the physical continuity of the city as they tie new construction to the city's past. This establishes a visual dialogue that vividly comments on the relationship of old and new buildings while it preserves the city as the physical emblem of human memory.

The character of this dialogue varies enormously. At one extreme infill building can produce stylistic uniformity as, for example, it has in the historic districts of American and European cities, where strict regulations govern the appearance of new buildings and require the rehabilation of old ones to match an established image of a previous epoch. In other cases, abstractly defined buildings, those more "modern" in appearance, can also knit together the historical fabric and contemporary urban situations. At its most pure, this kind of urbanism argues that the constant evolution of urban form requires equal treatment of the many architectural components of the central city and its suburbs, that one historical period should not be favored over another, and that infill building need not rely on stylistic means to re-establish urban continuity. Rather, and especially in the design of housing, it seeks to establish some kind of typological consistency with the exist-

*1*

*The East Harlem fabric c. 1950. The site for Lenox Terrace, a public housing housing project built by the New York City Housing Authority, is outlined behind the Abraham Lincoln Houses. Source: Committee on Slum Clearance Plans, Harlem: Slum Clearance Plan Under Title 1 of the Housing Act of 1949 (New York, January, 1951).*

ing situation or its historical context.[6] Different methods of producing infill housing also complicate the discussion, especially as the methods of producing infill building are confused with urbanistic attitudes. New construction, rehabilitation, or some combination of the two can reinforce existing urban patterns—either through stylistic repetition or through typological interpretation. Contextual requirements clearly influence the choice of method.[7]

Infill construction, even though it depends on the structure of the city as an essential given, still allows the improvement of the urban fabric at the building, the block, and the neighborhood scale. This kind of building reinforces the street and helps define a clear range of public, semi-public, and private spaces. These allow for increased neighborliness, social interaction, and personal safety. The spatial reinforcement of the character of individual streets and neighborhoods and the dependency on incremental rebuilding also encourage small-scale development and community participation in the development and management of buildings. In addition infill accepts improvement of buildings at the architectural scale, allowing, for example, innovations in the design of apartments, entry ways, stairs, and other semi-public spaces. Such interventions can occur on single blocks or in single buildings; they can also allow larger-scale general improvement. It is, however, difficult to use this process to radically alter the urban pattern of a neighborhood. Thus, if the neighborhood lacks large-scale public space, such as that found in public parks and gardens, the process of infill building cannot easily correct this problem. Rather, it mends what exists.

The program of the "Inner City Infill Competition" attempted to use infill housing to repair the fabric of central Harlem and provide social services needed by the community. A site with differently-sized lots and a variety of adjacent buildings and spaces required the design of several kinds of infill buildings suited to typical infill situations found in this part of New York City. These included a relatively simple party-wall building, larger groupings of buildings surrounding semi-public open spaces, and the rehabilitation of existing, run-down apartment buildings. The program also requested that new housing shelter the community's diverse social groups by asking for the design of apartment units for different sizes and kinds of families. It insisted on the improvement of the public and semi-public realms by requiring public spaces, civic amenities, commercial facilities, and parking. Though it stressed the advantages of the row house, it did not limit interpretation of infill to this building type. If anything, the required densities and open spaces suggested the reinterpretation of the row house and the incorporation of other, denser building types.[8]

In general the entries responded to two urban design strategies. One group, conceiving of the city block as an aggregate of separate, infill buildings, proposed to string these buildings along the streets of central Harlem. These designs most often used town house buildings to strengthen street walls and separate public and private space (Illus. 2). Other schemes augmented the space of the streets with sequences of public or semi-public spaces on the interior of the city blocks. Connecting one city block to another via new pedestrian or vehicular networks, this strategy generally required the use of more malleable apartment buildings to shape the public spaces, though at times townhouses were also employed (Illus. 3). Following the requirements of the competition, both groups used new construction, rehabilitation, or some combination of the two to achieve these ends (Illus. 4).

2
*"Inner City Infill Competition" entry*
*by J.C. Reynolds.*
*Elevation.*

3
*"Inner City Infill Competition" entry*
*by Hirsch/Danois Partnership.*
*Site plan.*

4
*"Inner City Infill Competition" entry*
*by Michael Pyatok.*
*Site plan.*

ELEVATION, 116th STREET    ELEVATION, 115th STREET

SECTION THROUGH SITE D. LOOKING NORTH

Each of these approaches to urban infill—that which sees the block as an aggregate of individual buildings focused on the street and that which concentrates on reshaping the city block to create a broader range of public and semi-public space—has been explored during the history of New York City's low-income housing as have the relative merits of using rehabilitation or new construction to create better housing stock. In order to better understand the advantages and disadvantages of each of these approaches to design and building, this essay will first discuss changing attitudes toward housing and urban reform during the nineteenth and twentieth centuries. It will then present examples of housing types in New York City that exemplify these specific attitudes towards urban infill, and it will close with a discussion of recent, successful examples of infill housing in other American and European cities. For the most part the discussion will present and analyze the formal intentions of designers and evaluate the resulting buildings.

During the eighteenth and nineteenth centuries the system of party-wall construction shaped the form of many western cities. In this kind of fabric the masonry walls of neighboring buildings touch each other, thus sharing side (commonly called "party") walls. These walls act as a fire barrier between buildings as well as providing major structural support. In New York City early party-wall buildings, usually called row or town houses, housed single families, sometimes on top of a family business; alternatively this form of building sheltered commercial activity. As with its Dutch and English precedents, the spanning potential of wooden beams (sixteen to twenty-five feet) determined the long, thin, shape of the New York building lot. This, in combination with high property values which encouraged dense land coverage, produced tall, narrow buildings and small rear yards. A small stoop often separated the two- to-three-room-deep buildings from the street, and an internal stair, perpendicular to the street, provided vertical circulation within the three-to-four story high buildings.[9] As the gridiron pattern came to structure the street network of the entire city new building types developed which incorporated party-wall construction. Tenements, apartment buildings, commercial buildings, and warehouses joined the original row house to form a physically continuous fabric.

Party-wall building[10] successfully produced cities whose continuous yet varied urban form clearly defined the public and private realms. For example, a row of simple town houses could easily define a public square; this with the addition of a gate or fence, could become a semi-public space. However, an individual row building did not easily adapt to the requirements of multi-family living and working because it could not easily form an adequately lit and ventilated apartment building or factory. In addition, based as it was on the principle of lot-by-lot development, the party-wall building could not efficiently shape shared gardens and courtyards on the interior of the block. Toward the end of the nineteenth century, urban reformers claimed that such shared gardens and courtyards were essential ingredients of the modern city, especially of its housing. Reducing urban density, they aired the fabric, provided gathering places sheltered from the street, and helped assure light, air, and cross-ventilation to building interiors.[11]

Even though many reformers rejected the individual party-wall building, they did accept the shape of the city. As the twentieth century progressed, texts such as

Ebenezer Howard's *Tomorrow: A Peaceful Road to Real Reform* and Le Corbusier's *Urbanisme*[12] supported the creation of new urban patterns to solve the problems of the nineteenth- century city. Their designs rejected many aspects of party-wall construction, favoring instead the reduction of urban congestion, the decentralization of central cities, and the zoning of the city into functionally distinct areas in order to improve its political, social, and economic functioning. Unsurprisingly, the designs did not foster physical continuity with the existing city whose problems had spawned them. Thus the garden city movement in England attempted to reduce London's size, comparing its growth to that of a "tumor,"[13] by developing satellite cities, limited in population, size, and density, in the surrounding countryside. The International Congress of Modern Architecture (C.I.A.M.), in *The Charter of Athens* written by Le Corbusier, argued that the city "no longer serves its function" since it suffers from "disorder" produced by "private initiatives inspired by personal interest and the lure of profit."[14] Rather, the *Charter* stressed a complete transformation of the European city, using enlightened centralized planning to let the city, now defined as an urban region, profit from the benefits of properly applied machine-age technology. After the Second World War applications of both of these philosophies altered the shape of every major American and European city and its suburbs despite the fact that in many cases the proposals were watered down by economic constraints, especially when the proposals involved public housing. This only exacerbated the problemmatic aspects of the original, theoretical proposals.[15]

From the beginning years of the modern movement on through the post World War II period, the provision of housing played a central role in the schemes for urban reform. As Le Corbusier said, "the building of [the] home, after more than a century of subjection to the brutal games of speculation, must become a humane undertaking."[16] Inspired by the idea of complete transformation of the urban environment, reformers on both sides of the Atlantic developed new housing types for the modern city. Freestanding apartment buildings, whether twenty-story point towers, ten-story slabs, or four-story bars, were sited to receive optimum sun exposure and to assure adequate light, air, and cross-ventilation (Illus. 5). Placed in open, generally green space, these methods of building attempted to reduce urban congestion by limiting ground coverage. For many reformers the technology of the machine age, which permitted the construction of high-rise buildings, also permitted the standardization of building elements. This, combined with idea of minimum living standards, held out hopes for reducing the cost of housing and promoting social equality. Regional planning, community, or public, control of the land, and government subsidy were also advocated as ways to reduce cost.[17]

Le Corbusier's and others' interest developed from need: European cities, in particular, experienced severe housing shortages due, in part, to the two world wars and the shift in population from rural to urban centers. In addition the modernist critique claimed that no other building type better exemplified the physical and social problems caused by the dense, continuous form of the industrial town than low- and moderate- income housing. The common housing types, the row house, tenement, and apartment building, relied on party-wall building to such an extent that they often did not provide adequately designed and ventilated apartments, did not offer adequate public space, especially courtyards and gardens to their residents, and when concentrated to maximum density, as in the working class districts of many industrial towns and cities, caused health and sanitation problems

5
*Lenox Terrace, New York, New York. c.*
*1950. Skidmore, Owings, and Merrill.*
*Site model. Source: Committee on Slum*
*Clearance Plans,* Harlem: Slum Clear-
ance Plan Under Title l *of the Housing*
*Act of 1949 (New York, Janaury, 1951).*

6
*The Commissioners' Plan, New York,*
*New York. 1811.*
*Source: John Reps,* The Making of
Urban America *(Princeton, N.J., 1965),*
*p. 298.*

5

6

for the city as a whole. In *Modern Housing*, Catherine Bauer castigated equally the "chaotic slum" of Park Avenue, the "mechanical slum," a late nineteenth-century middle-class suburb of London, and tenement housing, calling New York City's old-law tenement "the worst legalized building form in the world."[18]

Bauer's sentiments were not new; in fact they developed from nineteenth-century housing reform movements which concentrated on improving the urban housing of the working classes in Europe and the United States. Some reformers, such as Charles Fourier, the social theorist, and Robert Owen, the philanthropist, counseled abandoning the existing city altogether and creating new utopian communities. Others, by far the majority, accepted the concentration of urban populations in existing cities and set out to improve their housing stock. Conservative in their outlook, they accepted a limited public role, advocating at first simple government regulation of building that would establish minimum design standards for market-value housing, especially of tenements. Private building interests, however, bitterly resisted any form of control; and corrupt practices in municipalities that managed to pass legislation governing design produced only sporadic law enforcement. Alternatively, private philanthropic groups built model dwellings for low-income residents. By the beginning of the twentieth century, legislation in American and European cities had come to regulate the form of housing; moreover the legislation was enforced. Additionally, several cities, among them Paris, actively encouraged the private construction of model dwellings through tax incentives. At this point the efforts of a third group of reformers began to bear fruit. They insisted that governments enter the housing market and use public funds to build. This had occurred occasionally throughout the second half of the nineteenth century; Louis Napolon's construction of the Cit Napolon in Paris is a celebrated early example. Finally in 1893, the London County Council began to systematically construct public housing, setting the stage for large-scale government intervention in the twentieth century.[19]

In New York City a similar pattern of development has produced an urban fabric composed of a multitude of housing types, among them row houses, tenements, apartment buildings, towers, and slabs. The form of these buildings has developed in part from changing ideas toward policy and funding, a subject beyond the scope of this essay.[20] The building types have also developed as a consequence of the city's urban pattern. In 1811, The Commissioners' Plan divided the borough from 14th Street north to 155th Street into an evenly distributed grid of sixty-foot-wide streets and one-hundred-foot-wide avenues (Illus. 6). This simple gridiron form produced the typical Manhattan block, generally two hundred feet wide by eight hundred feet long. It, in turn, was divided into a smaller "gridiron" of building lots, each twenty-five by one hundred feet, chosen in part to suit the construction requirements of row houses. This dimension and, in the future, modules of it determined the basic building outline of tenements, apartment buildings, warehouses, and commercial buildings in Manhattan and nearby areas of the outer boroughs.

The Commissioners' Plan established a city pattern whose basic public space is the street. This occurred more for reasons of practicality and economic efficiency than as result of aesthetic sensibility. In order to provide as much land as possible for development, the plan designated the construction of one public park (what became Union Square) and very few public buildings for entire city's use. No space was given by the municipality to establish small residential squares such as had been created in other American and English cities.[21] This left the street as the city's prime public space, which the architectural pattern proposed by the Commissioners for each block also enforced. Each block consisted of butted, individual party-wall buildings. They strictly separated the private interior of the block from the public space of the street. In the interests of providing as much land as possible for development, no space on the block interior was allocated for semi-public use or for service alleys.

As many critics have noted, the size, shape, and orientation of the Manhattan gridiron blocks caused problems with light, air, and cross ventilation for housing types other than row houses.[22] The design of the old-law tenement quickly reveals them because it housed New York City's working population in denser construction than either the single-family town house or the row house converted to multi-family living could provide. Built on a lot-by-lot basis, these early apartment buildings maximized land value by covering individual lots as fully as possible, very often extending over ninety feet of their length. Containing as many as twelve rooms per floor, the inner rooms of these buildings could not receive light and air directly from the street or from a backyard. By 1879, legislation required the inclusion of small side courts, or light wells, to light and ventilate interior rooms of such buildings. Located at the service areas within the building, these produced the classic "dumbbell" shape of the old-law tenement (Illus. 7). Accepting the landlords' desire to produce buildings as densely as possible, in order to maximize profit, the law kept the size of the courts at a bare minimum. It did, however, limit lot coverage, require fire-escapes, and establish rudimentary sanitation standards.[23]

The strings of old-law tenements along the streets of the city's poorer neighborhoods created an urban fabric which, in the row house tradition, emphasized the street as public space. Entries to individual tenement buildings occurred either directly off the street or off of small stoops and articulated the solid street walls formed by these party-wall buildings. These walls also shut off the block interiors from the life of the street. Since the tenement-block interior lacked the private open space associated with row houses, the miniscule rear and side yards of the old-law tenements acted simply as light wells and service space, forcing activity to the street.

Ernest Flagg's 1894 tenement plan, which became the basis of legislation enacted in 1901, called the "New Law," modulated the strict separation of public and private space of the old-law tenement with small courtyard apartment houses. Flagg accepted the argument that the building coverage required on a twenty-five-by-one-hundred-foot lot to make profitable working-class housing could not provide adequately lit and ventilated apartments. He insisted that new tenements occupy at least two multiples of the standard lot. By limiting ground coverage to sixty-six per cent and establishing set-backs, his designs effectively prohibited the light well of the old-law tenement and made possible the collection of space into more generous, usable, semi-public courtyards, separated from the street by the mass of the new building (Illus. 8). The new four-bay building, that is a building on a hundred foot by a hundred foot lot, showed its clear debt to French precedent. Stairs, for example, leading to apartment units were entered only through the

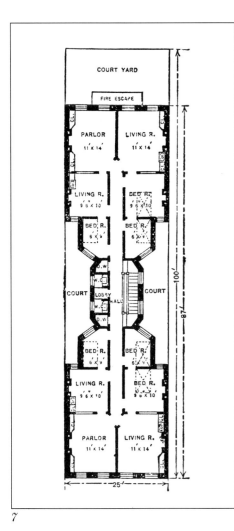

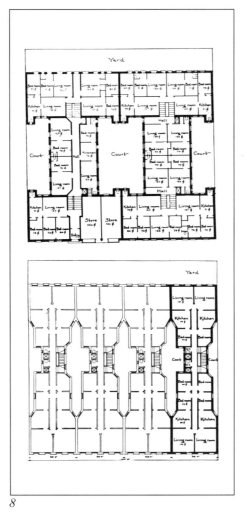

7
*Old-law tenement, New York, New York. James Ware. 1879.*
*Plan of winning entry to* Plumber and Sanitary Engineer *Competition.*
*Source: Robert DeForest and Lawrence Veilller (ed.),* The Tenement House Problem *(New York, 1903), vol. 1, p. 101.*

8
*Ernest Flagg's comparison of the new-law tenement and the old-law tenement.*
*Source:* The Architectural Review *10 (1903), p. 85.*

**9**
*Riverside Dwellings, Brooklyn, New York. William Field and Son. 1879. Perspective. Source: James Ford,* Slums and Housing *(New York, 1936), vol. 2, fig. 114.*

**10**
*Prince Albert Dwellings, London, England. Sir Henry Roberts. 1851. Plan and elevation. Source: John Nelson Tarn,* Five Percent Philanthropy *(Cambridge, 1973), p. 20.*

**11**
*Riverside Dwellings, Brooklyn, New York. William Field and Son. 1890. Ground level plan. Source: James Ford,* Slums and Housing *(New York, 1936), vol. 2, plate 6C.*

**12**
*Striver's Row, New York, New York. McKim, Mead and White. 1891-92. Site plan. Source: Leland Roth (ed.),* A Monograph of the Works of McKim, Mead, and White *(New York, 1977), p. 25.*

9

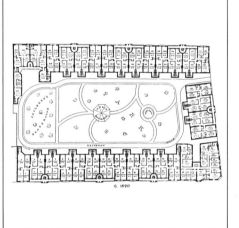
11

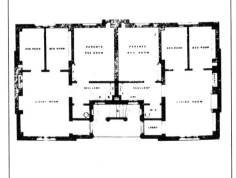
10

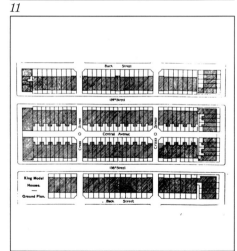
12

courtyard which was connected to the street by an arched passageway. Though the spaces of these courtyard buildings improved the lightwells associated with the old-law tenements, the tall, awkward proportions of the courtyard shut out sun from the court and apartment units on lower floors. In addition, Flagg continued to see the block as a string of individual infill buildings; rear and side yards did not shape a sequence of space on the interior of the block. Each courtyard remained the province of each building, and the street, rather than a spatial sequence internal to the block, continued to link buildings on the same block.[24]

The Warren Place Mews (1879) and the Riverside Dwellings (1890), built by A. T. White in Brooklyn, broke with the street-focused tenements to create semi-public space on the interior of the gridiron block. Using respectively the model of the mews and the perimeter block, the projects augmented the public space of the city's streets with a gridiron block designed as an entity in and of itself. Each block was served by internal spatial sequence and circulation. The Warren Place Mews, in effect, miniaturized the gridiron pattern to create a pedestrian green street on the interior of the block. The mews helped provide adequate light and air to the low-rise row-houses which form its edges and offered a space removed from the street for the use of its residents. The Riverside Dwellings (Illus. 9), a group of apartment buildings designed by William Field and Son, provided a large courtyard space on the interior of the block. It employed a type of apartment unit invented by Henry Roberts and developed by Sydney Waterlow in England. This type grouped two small apartment units around a common stair entered from the street and connected them with an open-air gallery to assure ventilation of the apartments and the public corridor (Illus. 10). Wet areas, toilets and kitchens with their plumbing, were expressly separated from the living spaces for health and sanitary reasons. They projected out the back of each apartment to assure adequate ventilation. The rest of the unit was two rooms deep, allowing light and air to reach directly into each living and sleeping room.[25]

Radically different from the apartment configurations found in old- and new-law tenements, this unit type permitted a linear arrangement of apartment clusters along a street front, as commonly occurred in its application in Great Britain, or around large, open courts, as, for example, in White's Riverside Dwellings. In this case, the two-room-deep ribbon of building, with the wet areas projecting out of the back facade, surrounded a large, semi-public garden (Illus. 11). It did not rely on developing the interior of the block to a maximum density on a lot-by-lot basis.[26] Still, since the building traced the shape of the existing urban pattern, it acted as a form of urban infill—simply on a larger scale than that of the individual building—that also provided significant semi-public space.

These last two projects of White, and to some extent, the courtyard version of the new-law tenement, took a very different attitude toward the street than that of the row house or the old-law tenement. By creating semi-public spaces on the interior of the block, each removed activity from the street and sheltered it in a courtyard or a through-block pedestrian street. This attitude, which also appeared in contemporary middle- and upper-income projects such as Striver's Row (1891-1892), a model row house project designed by McKim, Mead, and White (Illus. 12), and Graham Court (1901), a small perimeter block designed by Clinton and Russell (Illus. 13), began to question the traditional urban hierarchy of the New York street grid. The wall of housing no longer strictly separated the public space of

13
*Graham Court, New York, New York. Clinton and Russell. 1901. Perspective. Source:* Real Estate Record and Builders' Guide *73 (June 11, 1904), pp. 1464-73; or Robert A. M. Stern etal.,* New York 1900 *(New York, 1985), p 291.*

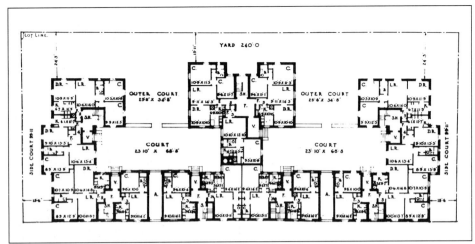

14
*Dunbar Apartments, New York, New York. Andrew Thomas. 1928. Typical floor plan. Source:* Architecture *59 (January 1929), p. 8.*

the street from the private space of rear yard or garden. Housing reformers advocated this approach for social and sanitary reasons. Seeing the street as a dangerous, at times evil place, they preferred the safety and cleanliness of the inner court and the advantages its form offered for bringing light and air into apartments. These courtyards, as they came to be used in low-, middle-, and upper-income projects in New York City during the first decades of the twentieth century, also provided collective spaces that helped establish an identity for each housing project. In some of the more elaborate perimeters, built either by labor unions, philanthropists, or private investors, the central courtyards offered beautiful gardens. Others remained paved courts. Still, as much as these projects challenged the hierarchy of the urban street network, they also maintained it, because the basic building outline respected the gridiron pattern. Neither accepting the urban status quo or denying it completely, they improved the city by transforming its block structure.[27]

Two of the better courtyard projects in New York City took very different apporaches toward the transformation of the New York City block. The Dunbar Apartment, designed by Andrew Thomas, was built by John D. Rockefeller, Jr. in 1928 for black middle-income residents, as a complex composed of cooperative apartments of various sizes, a day-care center, commercial space, and a bank. Occupying an entire city block, it preserved the street wall of central Harlem while providing a large, protected central garden space (Illus. 14). This space was entered from the street by passing through breaks in the six-story building. An articulated building wall in the inner courtyard created a series of smaller courts which were associated with entries into each of the apartment clusters (Illus. 15). Passages through the body of the building also connected the entry courts with the street. The articulation of the building wall permitted increased density and assured that the apartment units received adequate light and air.[28]

As much as the semi-public space of the Dunbar Apartments turned its back to the city, Harlem River Houses (1937), one of the first federally funded public housing projects built in New York City opened out to it. Designed by a team of architects headed by Archibald Manning Brown for low-income black residents, the project covered nine acres, the area of approximately three city blocks, near the Harlem River (Illus. 16). A broad central axis, previously East 152nd Street, linked a series of U-shaped courtyards from Macomb's Place across Seventh Avenue to a smaller housing complex on the banks of the Harlem River. Unlike Dunbar, the massing did not strictly conform to the city grid. Rather, in order to resolve the non-orthogonal geometry caused by Macomb's Place's running at a diagonal to the city grid, the massing set back from Macomb's Place and West 151st Street and established small courtyards which opened out to these streets. Already beginning to lose spatial definition, these courtyards, unfortunately, did not lead to apartment entries. The central pedestrian promenade, however, and the large courts adjacent to it, composed of a mixture of green and paved surfaces, provided clearly bounded, successful semi-public spaces. These, opening onto apartment entries, were accessible to the city at large.[29]

Harlem River Houses offered very well-designed apartments surrounded by useful and pleasing open spaces; however, the design's response to the basic outline of the city grid tempered its modernism with a respect for the form of the existing city. As the formal and economic arguments for building freestanding housing

15
*Dunbar Apartments, New York, New York. Andrew Thomas. 1928. Photograph of courtyard. Source:* Architecture *59 (January 1929), p. 7.*

16
*Harlem River Houses, New York, New York.*
*Archibald Manning Brown, etal. 1937.*
*Aerial perspective. Source: James Ford,*
Slums and Housing *(New York, 1936),*
*vol. 2, fig. 139b.*

17
*East River Houses, New York, New York. The New York City Housing Authority. 1941.*
*Aerial photograph. Source: The New York City Housing Authority,* East River Houses *(New York, 1941).*

16

17

gained credence, the New York City Housing Authority abandoned the approach it used in Harlem River Houses, an approach which depended on using a form of infill building. Rather, it accepted the necessity of radically altering the city fabric in order to provide new housing efficiently and economically.

In 1941, the Housing Authority built East River Houses, New York City's first public housing complex to use high-rise buildings, on a large superblock site at the western edge of the East River Drive (Illus. 17). This project, inspired as much by cost-cutting measures as by the idealism of the modern movement, revealed some of the problems associated with the careless insertion of free-standing buildings in a continuous city fabric. Six- to-ten story apartment buildings stood free amidst open green space and parking lots. The institutional character of the buildings, their unique shapes, x's, z's, and crosses, and their skew off the city grid to assure proper sun exposure isolated the buildings from the surrounding neighborhood. The geometry destroyed the public space of the street by removing one of its walls; it also made it impossible to establish clearly understood public spaces within the project. Moreover, poor site planning (to say nothing of the presence of the East River Drive) prohibited a strong visual connection of the project to the water. While the apartment units received adequate light and air, they were designed to minimum standard.[30]

For many architects and planners public housing projects came to symbolize what they perceived to be the failings of the modern movement's housing program. While accepting the desirability of providing affordable housing with flexible, well-designed apartments and nearby public and semi-public spaces, they questioned the isolation of the housing projects from the existing city fabric, the use of high-rise construction and superblock site planning, and the insistence on cost-cutting measures. Critics such as Jane Jacobs and Oscar Newman argued that architects and planners should seek inspiration from the existing urban fabric, generally formed in the nineteenth century, which clearly defined the public space of the street, the semi-public space of the courtyard, and the private space of the rear yard. Using low-rise infill building types, especially row houses and apartment houses, this kind of urban pattern produced a safer and more enjoyable environment than that found in slab-block and tower-in-the-park housing.[31] Though other critics argued that the problems of public housing were due as much, if not more, to the problems of an inadequate social structure,[32] the argument favoring respect for the urban context and the use of low-rise, high-density housing gained credence. Backing off from the idea that the provision of adequate housing depended on a complete transformation of the city's urban structure, designers began to reject the fragmentation and dispersal that urban renewal caused and argue for incremental repair of the city through the use of infill buildings and urban blocks.

Several low- and mid-rise projects in New York City, built during the 1960s and 1970s, reflect these changing attitudes. In Riverbend (Illus. 18), a successful middle-income cooperative built in Harlem along the East River, Davis, Brody and Associates responded to Alison and Peter Smithson's concept of the "street-in-the-air." Trying to tie the experience of circulation within buildings to the experience of the street, the Smithsons first proposed during the 1950s the use of exterior circulation galleries, or streets, to reach upper-level apartments. In Riverbend, the galleries, stacked on alternate floors of the L-shaped block, reach duplex

18
*Riverbend, New York, New York. Davis, Brody, and Associates. 1967. Apartment gallery. Source:* Architecture Plus *1 (November 1973), p. 65.*

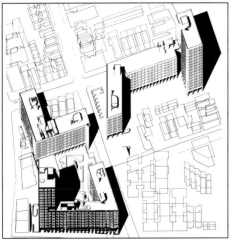

*19*
*Twin Parks North East, The Bronx,*
*New York. Richard Meier. 1976.*
*Site axonometric. Source:* Architecture
d'aujourd'hui *186 (August/September*
*1976), p. 5.*

apartments. Consciously modeled after town houses, even to the point of incorporating small stoops, the design of these apartments reinforced the raised street as a shared social space.[33]

In the late 1960s the New York State Urban Development Corporation (U.D.C.), speaking of the need for "urban infill," sponsored the construction of other new housing on scattered sites in the South Bronx. The massing of many of these projects, however, belied the intentions toward infill because the high-rise towers and mid-rise slabs remained quite distinct from the low-rise buildings of the adjacent neighborhoods (Illus. 19).[34] The Urban Development Corporation also sponsored the development of a low-rise prototype (Illus. 20) in conjunction with the Institute for Architecture and Urban Studies. In it rows of four-story interlocked duplex town houses were arranged according to a mews system in an attempt to maximize density while providing public, semi-public, and private space. A version of this prototype, Marcus Garvey Houses, was built in Brooklyn during the early 1970s.[35] In the Bronx, Ciardullo-Ehman Associates further developed the proposal they made to the U.D.C. competition, adapting the section of Le Corbusier's Marseilles Block apartment in order to create an efficient row house. It consisted of two apartment units, entered either directly from the street or from a shared public garden. Unlike the Marcus-Garvey project, which strictly separated public, semi-public, and private space, the Mott-Haven Infill project let the three overlap (Illus. 21).[36]

The rehabilitation and renovation of existing housing stock is another way to provide infill housing in New York City. Since it depends on the re-use of existing housing, its history has also been tied to the development of the city's urban pattern and has depended on changing attitudes toward policy and funding.[37] Like the construction of new housing, some rehabilitation focuses attention on the street as public space, while other examples augment the public space of the streets with other spatial sequences within the block. Most typically, the first approach involves the incremental repair of individual buildings.[38] However, renovation can perform more radical reconstruction of city blocks, using, for example, selective demolition of buildings and/or parts of buildings to create internal public spaces.

On the occasion of a competition sponsored by the New York State Reconstruction Commission in 1920 for the rehabilitation of a Lower East Side block Andrew Thomas and Robert Kohn exchanged differing views on the feasibility of housing rehabilitation. In an article published in the *Architectural Record*,[39] Thomas argued that the old-law tenement was "miserably deficient" in design and in construction and the new-law tenement was already outmoded. Given the "increased cost of construction and improved living standards," it was time to "put tenement housing on a new basis." He found fault with the premises of the competition (Illus. 22), arguing that it would be less expensive to build new buildings than renovate older ones. These, since they required less building coverage, would provide a better living environment (Illus. 23). Kohn, however, argued that it was highly unlikely that either the government or the private sector would remove the 50,000 existing tenements and replace them with new and better housing. It would simply cost too much. Rather than ignoring these buildings and abandoning their residents economical renovation should be undertaken. Adjacent buildings should be

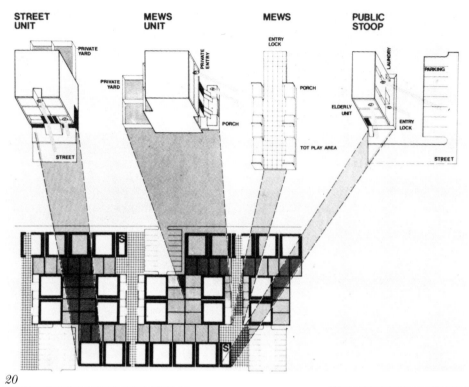

STREET UNIT · MEWS UNIT · MEWS · PUBLIC STOOP

20

21

20
*Prototype for Marcus Garvey Houses, Brooklyn, New York. Institute for Architecture and Urban Studies. 1973. Analytical axonometric of unit types. Source:* Architecture d'aujourd'hui *186 (August/September 1976), p. 16.*

21
*Mott-Haven Infill, The Bronx, New York. Ciardullo, Ehman, Associates. 1974.*
*Photograph of courtyard. Source: Architect.*

22
*Winning entry, New York State Reconstruction Commission Competition. Sibley and Fetherston. 1920. Typical floor plan. Source:* The Architectural *Record 48 (November 1920), p. 419.*

23
*Proposal criticizing premises of New York State Reconstruction Commission Competition. Andrew Thomas. 1920. Typical floor plan. Source:* The Architectural Record *48 (November 1920), p. 421.*

24
*First Houses, New York, New York. The New York City Housing Authority. 1935. Site perspective. Source: James Ford,* Slums and Housing *(New York, 1936), vol. 2, fig. 138b.*

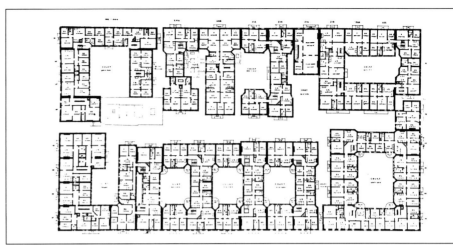

22

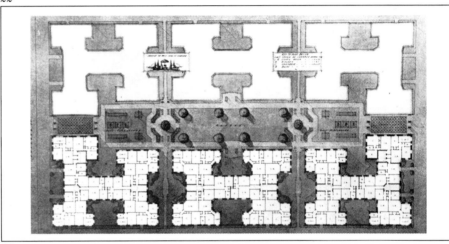

23

24

combined and portions, especially on the interior of the block, demolished in order to assure proper lot coverage.

The New York City Housing Authority, in its first project, called appropriately First Houses, built in 1936, followed this procedure, though for financial reasons rather than from an ideological commitment to renovation (Illus. 24). In this project the complete overhaul of an L-shaped group of old-law tenements, located on the Lower East Side, maintains the street wall of East Third Street and Avenue A while creating open space within the block interior. Neighboring tenements, gutted and joined into one building, share a new stair, service core, and apartment units; the extraction of every third tenement assures light and air to the interior rooms of the new, free-standing housing blocks. Along East Third Street shared gardens alternate with entry patios which lead to a rear, semi-public courtyard. On the avenue, new one-story stores occupy these spaces.[40] Federal subsidies became available for constructing new housing in the late 1930s, and the Housing Authority fully embraced the philosophy of slum clearance, abandoning what little interest it had had in using rehabilitation to provide housing. Though studies continued to examine the feasibility of using rehabilitation to provide low-income housing,[41] it was not until the 1960s that a renewed interest in housing rehabilitation developed. Growing out of the advocacy planning and community preservation movements,[42] those favoring rehabilitation augmented the arguments used in the 1920s. These had stated that it makes economic, social, and aesthetic sense to repair the fabric of the city by combining and redesigning the interiors of buildings. The new argument added symbolic and political dimension by saying that the restoration and repair of communities, building by building, symbolizes the local community's strength and identity, especially when tenant cooperatives and community development organizations sponsor it. In addition, they proposed using sweat equity to rehabilitate housing. This process, conceived of as a way to lower construction costs, allowed residents to earn a place to live by their own effort, or "sweat;" usually it involved teaching construction skills.[43]

Some of the more successful rehabilitation projects in New York have been sponsored by the Manhattan Valley Development Corporation, an development organization formed by the residents of Manhattan Valley, a working class community along the northern and western edges of Central Park. One of their first efforts used federal subsidies to rehabilitate five old-law tenements and one large apartment building on the corner of 104th Street and Manhattan Avenue, two streets adjacent to Frederick Douglas Houses, a large tower-in-the-park public housing project. The renovation, designed by Levenson-Thaler Associates (1980), maintains existing lot coverage (Illus. 25). However, a common hallway running through what were once the light wells closest to the street, joins the interiors of the tenements and connects each to a shared elevator. In both buildings apartments, redesigned to suit the needs of larger families, house significantly fewer people than those of the original buildings. Thus the project reduces density without reducing lot coverage and without significantly changing the surrounding urban environment, except of course, through its repair of the fabric. Neither does it provide any semi-public outdoor space; rather it relies on the street and public spaces in the adjacent public housing project to satisfy this need.[44]

As successful as this and other projects have been, a bias, similar to that which informed the first slum clearance plans, remains against tenement rehabilitation.

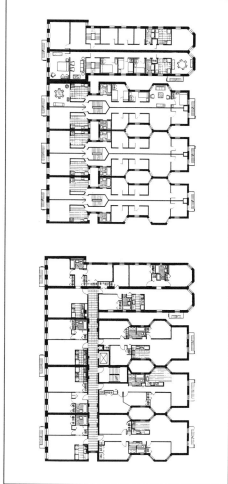

25
*104th Street Housing Renovation, New York, New York. Levenson-Thaler Associates, 1980.*
*Ground floor plan before and after renovation. Source: Architect.*

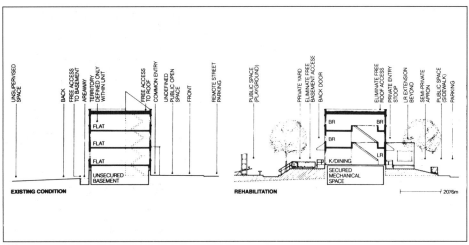

26
*Commonwealth Development, Boston, Massachusetts. Tise Wilhelm, and Associates, and Carr-Lynch Associates. 1983-1986.*
*Building sections before and after renovation. Source:* Progressive Architecture *67 (May 1986), p. 95.*

Critics point out that rehabilitation, especially of old-law tenements, prohibits the provision of adequate semi-public spaces both on the exterior and the interior of buildings and restricts the design of the apartments, making it difficult to size and dispose rooms with sufficient light, air, and ventilation. In addition it costs nearly as much to completely renovate a tenement as it does to build new housing.[45]

Advocates of rehabilitation, on the other hand, hold that it does offer a reasonable alternative to new construction in part because moderate rehabilitation is less expensive than new building. In addition, the incremental reconstruction of older structures, in neighborhoods made up of nineteenth and early twentieth century fabric buildings interspersed with post-war slabs and towers, retains the community's ties to its past. The process may not generate additional public and semi-public space; but such spaces already exist in abundance in these communities usually in the post-war housing projects. While it may be difficult to achieve apartments with large, well-lit rooms, the buildings do have certain architectural amenities which new buildings often lack, and their smaller scale helps engender a neighborly street life.[46] Thus rehabilitation is valuable not so much because it saves older buildings but because of the improvement in the urban environment it can make.

Renovation as a form of urban infill is not restricted to nineteenth century tenements; the vast majority of the nation's public housing projects, constructed during the 1950s and 1960s, now require it.[47] Since the New York City Housing Authority's waiting list consists of over 165,000 families, it faces little immediate pressure to dramatically change the projects it either owns or manages. Here, the renovation of public housing has consisted mostly of smaller-scale improvements, such as window replacement. However, theoretical projects have proposed using infill building to integrate the city's high rise housing projects into the adjacent city fabric. These projects intersperse small-scale infill buildings between existing towers and slabs to reestablish street walls and to clearly define semi-public spaces on the interiors of super-block projects. Applying ideas discussed by Jacobs and Newman, the proposals suggest tying the high-rise buildings to the ground through the use of street-entered units and landscaping. The renovations also incorporate units designed for large families.[48]

In American cities other than New York, public housing authorities have begun to implement proposals for improving the design of low- and high-rise projects. In many cases these projects use principles similar to those that inspired the earlier, theoretical proposals. The new site designs seek to integrate the superblock projects more closely into the communities which surround them by creating a broader range of public, semi-public, semi-private, and private spaces on the interior and exterior of the projects. This is often achieved by constructing new infill buildings which reestablish exterior street walls and create more clearly defined internal courtyard spaces. It is accompanied by rehabilitation of the housing units which adapt apartments to the needs of the larger families and more permanent population that now inhabit public housing.[49]

The Boston Public Housing Authority's work in this regard has been remarkable.

Acknowledged as a crisis-ridden agency by the late 1970s, a court order, following a class action suit brought by tenants, required the Authority to improve both the physical condition of its housing stock and its management procedures.[50] Faced with housing that was only seventy-five percent inhabited the Authority worked with tenant organizations during the late 1970s and early 1980s to develop proposals that reduced density in such projects as Franklin Field, West Broadway, Columbia Point, and Fidelis Way. In general, the Authority relied on rehabilitating the existing housing blocks to make bigger apartments for larger families, to improve the block's physical relationship to adjacent open spaces, and to upgrade the design of shared interior spaces and services, especially public circulation. Site improvements, such as running the street grid through the projects, redesigning public spaces, private spaces, and parking, and upgrading community services, helped to establish clear, spatial hierarchies and circulation within the sites, and to lessen the institutional character of the projects, better integrating them into the surrounding communities (Illus. 26).[51]

Some of the Boston projects relied on the demolition of portions of the existing housing to reduce project densities and provide needed space for community services. The transformation of Fidelis Way into Commonwealth Development, designed by Tise, Wilhelm, and Associates and Carr-Lynch Associates, required the destruction of two housing blocks along with renovation of the remaining housing and site improvements (Illus. 27). This created space for a new community management building, a new day-care center, and gardens. At Columbia Point, which had experienced vacancy rates of close to sixty-five percent prior to proposals to change it to a new community called Harbor Point, seventeen of the thirty original mid- and low-rise buildings were destroyed (Illus. 28), making room for site improvements and the construction of new low-rise housing. The new site plan, designed by a team of architects headed by Goody-Clancy Associates, gives the buildings fronts and backs by orienting them to a street network, derived from the adjacent neighborhood's grid pattern, and a broad mall providing a vista over Boston Harbor (Illus. 29). The area is served by stores and community and day-care centers. The positioning of the new housing and the design of the street pattern creates small, semi-public pedestrian courtyards, each serviced by vehicular streets. The use of pitched roofs and varied materials and window types will give the new and rehabilitated housing a domestic image.

As Antonio di Mambro points out in an enlightening article in *Space and Society*, the Boston Housing Authority and the Columbia Point Task Force, the project's tenant organization, conceived of the Columbia Point transformation as a program which "would create a major racially and economically integrated urban residential community."[52] Working in concert, the two groups proposed partially subsidizing the site's improvement by the private market. Thus the new project, when completed, will provide four hundred units (approximately one-third of the one thousand four hundred total) for low-income housing with the balance divided between moderate and market-value housing. A private development company, consisting of representatives of the tenant group and a private developer, will oversee the construction of a wide variety of unit types, ranging from newly constructed three-story townhouses to duplexes and simplexes in renovated apartment buildings. It will also own and manage the completed complex.

Certain troubling questions persist at Columbia Point, even though the goals of

27
*Commonwealth Development, Boston, Massachusetts. Tise Wilhelm and Associates and Carr-Lynch Associates. 1983-1986.*
*Site plan. Source: NYSCA.*

*28*

*Harbor Point, Boston, Massachusetts.*
*Goody, Clancy, etal. 1978-1990*
*(projected).*
*Site plan before and after renovation.*
*Source:* Progressive Architecture *67*
*(May 1986), p. 97.*

*29*

*Harbor Point, Boston, Massachusetts.*
*Goody, Clancy. etal. 1978-1990*
*(projected).*
*Bird's eye perspective. Source:* Progressive Architecture *67 (May 1986), p. 97.*

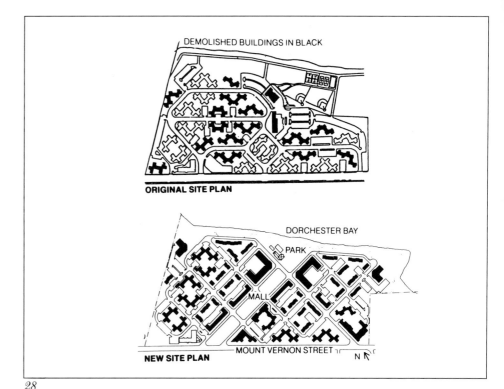

*28*

*29*

creating a mixed community are admirable. It remains to be seen whether the new project can overcome the social stigma originally attached to living in Columbia Point and whether the site's isolated location will attract the racial, social, and economic mix upon which its financing and design are based. Tenant participation in the development process did assure a higher standard of living for the original low-income residents who chose to remain; however, the improved standard occurred at a high cost—the removal of units once used by low-income tenants. Presumably the people who originally lived in these apartments need housing of as good quality as those remaining in Columbia Point will receive; yet the units converted for middle- and upper-income use were not replaced with low-income apartments elsewhere. Future proposals for turning public housing projects into racially, socially, and ethnically mixed housing will need to solve this problem.

In some American cities the construction of new infill housing by the public and private sectors has augmented the process of reconstruction, albeit in very modest numbers. Most of this new infill housing for low- and moderate-income families has sought to deinstitutionalize the image of public housing, very often, equating an institutional image with that of a high-rise apartment building.[53] This and a desire to integrate the new low-income housing into existing site conditions has often led designers to propose the incremental repair of fragmented urban fabric by building new town houses and detached single-family homes. This tends to create a fabric which stresses the street as public space. In the Andrew Square Project, designed by William Rawn and Associates for the Bricklayers and Laborers Non-Profit Housing Company in 1986, eighteen two-story townhouses mend a gap on a Boston street lined with two-story one- and two-family houses (Illus. 30). Steven Winters Associates developed two- and three-bedroom houses for infill sites in Asbury Park, New Jersey (see illus. 34). This project, winner of a Department of Housing and Urban Development (H.U.D.) honor award in 1986, draws on the freestanding one- and two-family houses in the surrounding neighborhood.[54] Another scatter-site project, also a winner of a H.U.D. honor award in 1985, has been built in Charleston, South Carolina (see illus. 32). In this project the Charleston Housing Authority, using H.U.D. subsidies received before the Reagan administration slashed the housing budget, built one hundred thirteen units of housing. Almost all of these were modeled on the city's standard house type: a long, thin building with side and front porches, whose form, responding to the sub-tropical climate, evolved to help increase the flow of air through the dwelling.[55] And in Berkeley, the Lyndon-Buchanan project for the University Avenue Housing Cooperative (1982) mixes the construction of town houses and apartment buildings with the rehabilitation of bungalows and an existing apartment building. In this project several mid-block mews connect the different housing types. Their site placement reflects similar kinds of housing and massing in the immediate neighborhood (Illus. 31).[56]

The architectural expression of each of these projects successfully challenges the anonymous and institutional image usually associated with low-income housing and helps to successfully integrate the new buildings into adjacent neighborhoods. In Charleston the Housing Authority first chose a scatter-site approach because various infill sites were cleared and available for construction. Once this decision was made, the Authority insisted on building housing that was "compatible with the existing neighborhood."[57] After a long research period the architects, Bradfield Associates and Middleton McMillian Architects, independently developed schemes that reinterpreted Charleston's traditional single-family house as

*30*
*Andrew Square, Boston, Massachusetts. William Rawn and Associates. 1986.*
*Site axonometric. Source: Architect.*

*31*
*University Avenue Housing Cooperative, Berkeley, California. Lyndon-Buchanan. 1982.*
*Ground floor plan of complex showing context.*
*Source: Architect.*

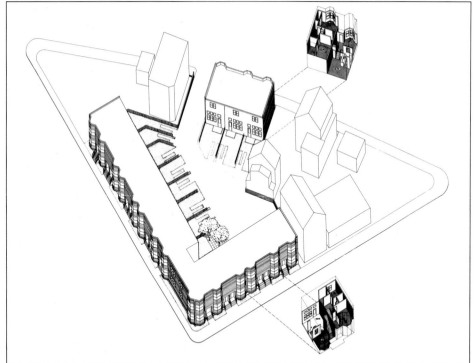

30

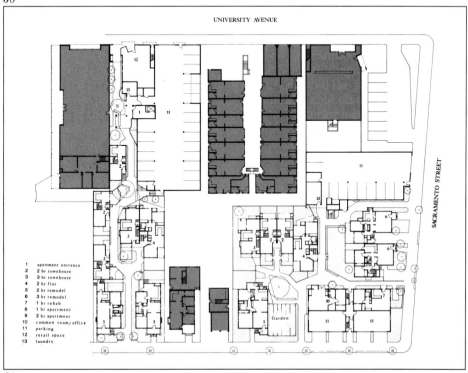

31

two-family duplexes similar in materials, scale, and form to the original house type (Illus. 32). Similarly the Boston, Asbury Park, and Berkeley projects, each using infill as the basic design premise, architecturally responded to their adjacent neighborhoods in order to avoid the banality of many public housing projects (Illus. 33). In the as yet unbuilt Asbury Park project, windows, materials, and roof shapes echo those of the neighboring houses (Illus. 34). In the Berkeley project, more modernist than the others in expression, massing changes address different site conditions. Again, porches, sloped roofs, and stoops tie the buildings to the context.

Repairing the city by constructing individual buildings, these projects do not, for the most part, create new, identifiable, public gathering space. This contrasts with the renovations of public housing projects which offer, in many cases, public and semi-public courtyards and gardens. However the incremental repair of the urban fabric does contribute to the definition of a larger public realm. In the Boston, Asbury Park, and Charleston examples the free-standing single-family and attached row houses help articulate and define the street's public space by re-establishing the street wall (Illus. 35). In addition, the large porches and stoops in all three designs buffer the public space of the street and the private space of the house with spaces that enrich the street experience and encourage neighborliness and social interaction. In the Berkeley project the interior mews do give some semi-public space to the project. However, this is kept to an absolute minimum in order to increase the size of private gardens. Here too, porches and stoops establish a buffer zone between the street, mews, and house (Illus. 36).

In contrast to the paucity of government-sponsored low-income housing renovation and construction in the United States, European governments have continued to subsidize the rehabilitation and construction of housing in such countries as Germany, France, The Netherlands, Italy, Spain, and even Margaret Thatcher's Great Britain during the past decade.[58] Correspondingly, designers and the public have accepted infill building as one way to provide low-to-moderate income housing in central cities and near-lying suburbs.[59] As in the United States these projects use new construction, rehabilitation, or some combination of the two to strengthen the structure of the existing city. This process, because it uses low-rise high-density housing types, clarifies the relationship between public, semi-public, semi-private, and private spaces in existing fabric disrupted by urban renewal, building abandonment and decay, and other consequences of poor planning. It also addresses the quality of the individual's dwelling, allowing for improved light and air, apartment design, and semi-public areas.

As in the United States the process occurs at the scale of individual buildings, urban blocks, and neighborhoods. In addition, designers respond to design strategies comparable to those used in the United States even though the structure of the European urban fabric can differ enormously from that found in American cities. They treat the block as an aggregate of separate infill buildings, stressing the street as the prime public realm. Alternatively, they conceive of the block (or, depending on the size of the site, segments of the block) as the principle morphological element of the city which provides a variety of shared spaces separate from the street. The differing physical and cultural milieus in continental and English cit-

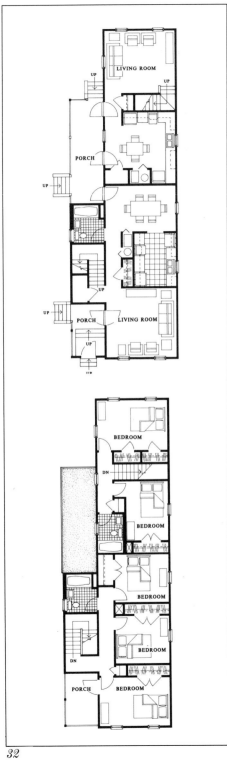

LIVING ROOM

UP

PORCH

UP

UP

UP

PORCH  LIVING ROOM

UP

DN

BEDROOM

DN

BEDROOM

BEDROOM

BEDROOM

DN

PORCH  BEDROOM

35

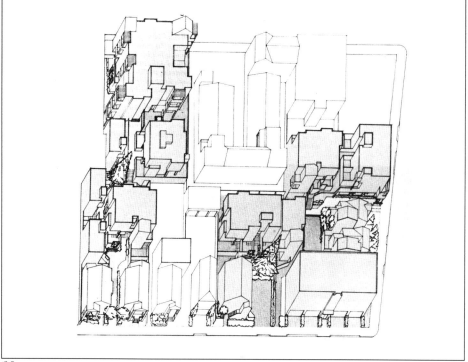

36

*37*
*Infill Housing, Hackney, London,*
*England. Colquhoun and Miller. 1983.*
*Street elevation. Source:* Architectural
Design *354 (1984), p. 85.*

*38*
*Infill Housing, Hackney, London,*
*England. Colquhoun and Miller. 1983.*
*Site plan. Source: NYSCA.*

*39*
*Infill Housing, Hackney, London,*
*England. Colquhoun and Miller. 1983.*
*Apartment plans. Source:* Architec-
tural Design *54 (1984), p. 86.*

*37*

ies, however, engender the use of different types of buildings. The row house, with its image of single-family living, dominates work in Great Britain, as it does in the United States, and the apartment house, usually built around a courtyard and formed to house families and individuals collectively, appears more frequently on the continent.[60] In addition, the form of European historical town centers, especially those on the continent which have been formed by centuries of aggregate growth, encourages architects to think typologically, that is, to create contemporary analogues of historical building types.[61] The best housing in these countries does not simply reuse the traditional definition of a housing type. Rather, typological transformations allow the architects to address urban fabric composed of a multitude of building types, to say nothing of the social and cultural needs of their late twentieth century inhabitants. This can create infill housing which appears as "modern" as that which it criticizes, the free-standing slabs and towers of the 1950s and 1960s.[62]

In Britain, those projects which use the row house model tend to accept its traditional separation of the public and private realms. Colquhoun and Miller's infill housing in Hackney, London (1983) responds to the massing of nearby semi-detached buildings, as it recalls the historical precedent of Henry Roberts' Prince Albert Houses (see illus. 10). It pairs two row houses around a large shared porch which is separated from the street by a small stoop (Illus. 37). The three-story buildings, topped with pitched roofs, either stand free, surrounded by small side yards, or in attached rows of butted buildings (Illus. 38). On the interior, the buildings can offer two ground level flats topped with two duplex apartments or two three-story walk-ups (Illus. 39). Whatever the interior combinations of units, the elevations do not reveal explicitly the inner functioning of the building. Nor do they adjust to changing site conditions. Rather, each block remains autonomous, giving uniformity to the street experience.[63]

Also in London, Jeremy Dixon's combination of building types on Ashmill Street, Paddington (1984), mends a hole in the fabric while incorporating necessary site amenities. Sponsored by the Westminster City Council, this project offers the possibility of home ownership to moderate-income occupants of public housing. It groups six row houses into a continuous terrace that breaks to accommodate a parking lot toward the corner of the street (Illus. 40). A small three-story apartment house, with two apartments per floor, terminates the block (Illus. 41). Each of the terrace's houses consists of a duplex apartment and a basement flat that require finishing by the occupants. In this case, the entries are not shared; rather the upper duplex unit is entered directly from the street by means of a small stair, and a separate stair gives entry to the lower-level apartment. Here, manipulation of the elevations, especially the use of alternating bands of rendered stucco and brick, tie the project to the context. Similar to the vertical element of Colquhoun and Miller's two-story porch, tall, thin windows articulate the predominantly horizontal facade.[64]

In these two projects constraints of budget and site have produced small, even minimally-sized apartments in buildings which make great effort to look like the traditional, inwardly-focused single-family row house (as indeed the Hackney project can be).[65] Still, aspects of each project's street elevation gesture out to the street's public space and enliven the street more than the traditional row house normally does. This extension of the building into the street perceptually expands

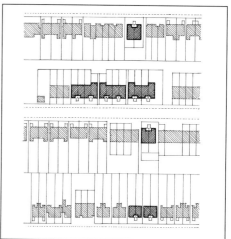

*38*

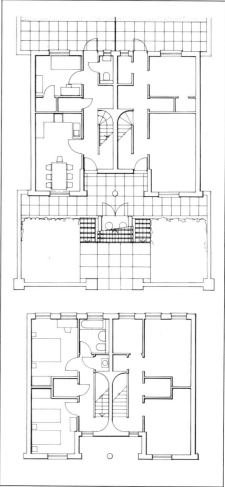

*39*

**65**

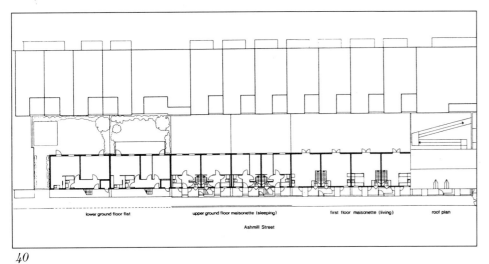

40

lower ground floor flat          upper ground floor maisonette (sleeping)          first floor maisonette (living)          roof plan

Ashmill Street

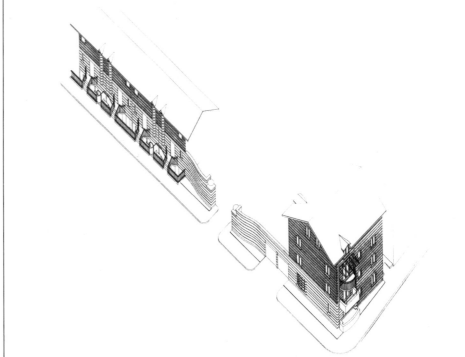

41

42

43

40
*Infill Housing, Ashmill Street, London, England. Jeremy Dixon. 1984. Site plan. Source: NYSCA.*

41
*Infill Housing, Ashmill Street, London, England. Jeremy Dixon. 1984. Site axonometric. Source:* The Architects' Journal *182 (2 October 1985), p. 23.*

42
*Infill Housing, Ashmill Street, London, England. Jeremy Dixon. 1984. Photograph of street. Source: Architect.*

43
*Infill Housing, Hackney, London, England. Colquhoun and Miller. 1983. Photograph of street. Source:* Architectural Design *54 (1984), p. 84.*

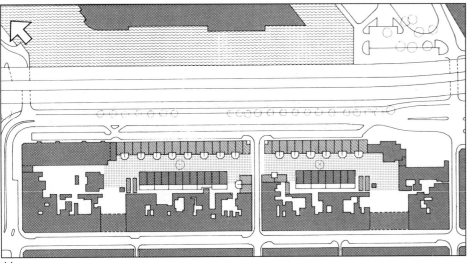

44
*Haarlemmer Houtuinen, Amsterdam,*
*The Netherlands. Herman Hertzberger*
*and Van Herk and Nagelkerke.*
*1978-82.*
*Site plan. Source:* NYSCA.

45
*Haarlemmer Houtuinen, Amsterdam,*
*The Netherlands. Herman Hertzberger*
*and Van Herk and Nagelkerke. 1978-*
*82.*
*Photograph of street. Source:* Architecture d'aujourd'hui *225 (February 1983),*
*p. 57.*

46
*Haarlemmer Houtuinen, Amsterdam,*
*The Netherlands. Van Herk and*
*Nagelkerke. 1978-1982.*
*Photograph of elevation. Source:* Archi-
tecture d'aujourd'hui *225 (February*
*1983), p. 61.*

the space of the apartments. In the Dixon project, tall narrow bay windows give light to the stair and the living room and strongly connect these spaces to the street (Illus. 42). They also help identify the entry to the basement apartment. In the Colquhoun and Miller project, the recessed two-story porch gives an outside foyer to each house block (Illus. 43). In this case the taut exterior building wall and the monumental space of the porch prevent views into the house and clearly mark the boundary between the public life of the street and the private life of the dwelling. Still, both of these moves enrich the life of the street, even though the buildings themselves do not define any other public or semi-public space.

As much as row house projects such as these reinforce the traditional separation of the private interior of the block from the public space of the street, this housing type can also be manipulated to provide semi-public space on the interior of a city block. Since this design strategy inverts the public/private relationship normally found in row housing, it usually requires the housing to turn its back to the existing street and focus on the space internal to the block. Often such projects draw on the imagery of the mews to create linear, street-like pedestrian spaces for the block interior from which the buildings are entered.

In Amsterdam, Herman Hertzberger and Van Herk and Nagelkerke have used this model to link the ragged fragments of two adjacent blocks exposed by the construction of a highway. The internal pedestrian street, called Haarlemmer Houtuinen, provides semi-public space open only to pedestrian traffic. The new housing, designed between 1978 and 1982 (Illus. 44) consists of the common pattern of butted row houses, each unit composed of two street-entered ground floor apartments topped by a pair of duplexes entered from a shared stair (Illus. 45). However, unlike the Dixon and Colquhoun and Miller projects in London, these buildings look more like apartment houses than single-family homes. This collective reading, which certainly draws on the imagery of Dutch housing built earlier in this century,[66] helps to reinforce the pedestrian street as the residents' major public space. All apartments are entered off the new pedestrian street which the kitchens, dining areas, and adjacent balconies face.

As much as the architects respect the constraints of the site plan, each one differently interprets the nature of the pedestrian street. In the Van Herk and Nagelkerke project the three-story buildings step back slightly as they rise. This increases the amount of sun able to reach the interior street and small balconies which cluster around the shared stair to the upper-level apartments (Illus. 46). Despite this slight terracing, the closed street wall separates internal movement through the buildings from movement on the street. This makes this side of the street more similar to a street of traditionally defined row houses than those on the opposite side.

Hertzberger's design strategy opens up the facade of the building facing an internal public space to the life in that space. This more typically occurs in courtyard apartment buildings than in row housing because this type of housing shelters its public, semi-public, or semi-private spaces from the street, allowing more interpretation of form of the public realm. Hertzberger, however, takes advantage of the row housing's interior prospect to relax the facade facing the pedestrian street (Illus. 47). Thus the massing of the four-story buildings engages building circulation and exterior space with movement on the street. Balconies at the third story

45

46

47
*Haarlemmer Houtuinen, Amsterdam, The Netherlands. Herman Hertzberger. 1978-1982.*
*Photograph of elevation. Source: Architect.*

sit on tall brick piers which create an arcade in front of the building's facade. The arcade shelters metal stairs that give access to upper level duplexes; the street level gardens and unit entries also occur in this space.[67]

Perimeter blocks, low-rise apartment houses built around shared courtyards, have occurred historically and have been proposed for American and English cities; however, they occur more frequently on the continent, where small-scale courtyard apartment houses make up the historical fabric of most European cities. In part this is because the relatively large depth of continental urban blocks required courtyards to bring light and air into the middle of the block, especially when covered to maximum density during the nineteenth and early twentieth centuries. Additionally, nineteenth-century European culture supported the type of public life implied by the building type.[68] In the interest of knitting new projects into the context and of creating shared spaces separate from the street, many contemporary designers repeat these housing forms. For example, several of the projects produced in conjunction with the Internationale Bauausstellung (I.B.A.) in Berlin take this approach with J.P. Kleihues' Block 270, Alvaro Siza's Bonjour Tristesse, and O.M. Ungers' project on the Lutzoplatz being three notable examples. In France Ricardo Bofill has also used the perimeter block housing type on larger-scale infill sites in Paris and Montpelier.[69]

Whether constructed on party-wall sites or on cleared blocks, the form of the courtyard apartment house extends the spatial qualities of the "out-of-doors city" into the interior of the block. This produces "sitting rooms" for the building's or block's residents, analogous to the larger city's squares and plazas.[70] Inevitably this produces a tension between the courtyard and the street. The size of the design proposals has important consequences for both. Smaller-scale buildings produce multiple building and/or courtyard entries along the street. As with row housing, these buildings tend to reinforce the existing street as the residents' major public space. Correspondingly, the courtyard spaces in these buildings, smaller and more intimate in quality, work best when they become semi-public, semi-private, or at times, even private space.

Antoine Grumbach's apartment house along the Quai des Jemmapes in Paris (1984-1986) reveals the tensions between the street front and courtyard space that exist in smaller-scale courtyard building. Constructed as part of the city of Paris' recent effort to build low-income housing and services in the eastern portion of the city,[71] it, like the traditional Parisian apartment house, is a mixed-use building which maintains the street wall and surrounds an internal courtyard. Street entries reach a community center on the first two floors and housing above; workshops are entered off a courtyard at the rear of the building. These sit over a basement gymnasium. Making major frontal gestures to the quai, the building helps knit together a portion of the street wall at a critical junction along the Canal St. Martin. Just as the canal takes a sharp bend, a lot, cleared by urban renewal, separates a nineteenth-century block and a post-war apartment building which is set back from the street wall (Illus. 48). In order to tie this fabric together, two segments of the new building align with the adjacent buildings, and a large semi-circular entry hall joins them. The elevations help to resolve the visual shear between the buildings. A brick screen, forming the facade's first layer,

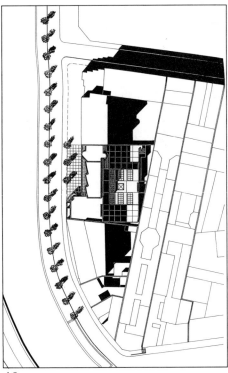

48
*Apartment House. Quai des Jemmapes, Paris, France. Antoine Grumbach. 1984-1986. Site plan. Source: NYSCA.*

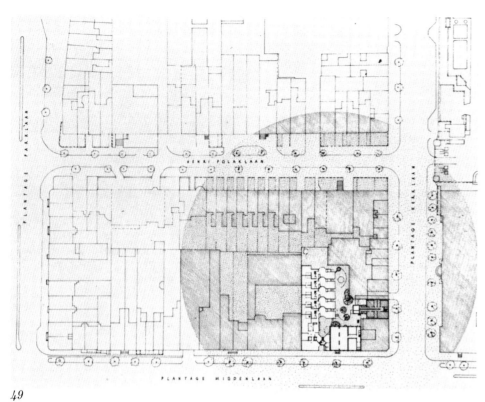

49

50

49
*Mothers' House, Amsterdam, The Netherlands. Aldo Van Eyck. 1974-1980. Site plan. Source: NYSCA.*

50
*Mothers' House, Amsterdam, The Netherlands. Aldo Van Eyck. 1974-1980. Photograph of street. Source:* The Architectual Review *17l (March 1982).*

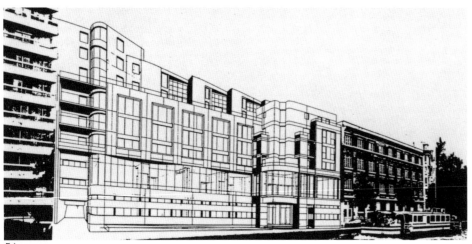

51
*Apartment House, Quai des Jemmapes,
Paris, France. Antoine Grumbach.
1984-1986.
Photomontage of street. Source:* Lotus
*41, p. 103.*

seems to peel away at the entry lobby to reveal the second layer of white tiles which rises to cover the upper floors of the entire building. Double high terraces on the second-floor community space also tie both sections of the building together. The courtyard, however, seems torn between serving as representational semi-public space and acting as a private backyard. Certainly the strength of the quai elevation, the size of the courtyard and its separation from the major circulation system of the building suggest it would be more suitably developed as a private or semi-private space than as the semi-public space it now is.[72]

In the Mothers' House (1974-1980), the ambivalence of the courtyard building's relationship with the street pervades Aldo Van Eyck's design for a shelter for homeless mothers and children in Amsterdam. The sponsoring organization, Hubertus Association, wanted to expand its facilities located in a midblock nineteenth-century apartment building. After demolition of a portion of the existing structure, a new, steel-framed, L-shaped building (Illus. 49) was built, separating the living quarters of mothers and children. Van Eyck placed the children's living and play space in a new two-story nursery wing which extends into the private garden, the literal courtyard of the project. At the street, the new wing rises to five stories and is joined to the old masonry townhouse with a brightly colored transparent stair which opens the life of the building's community onto the street (Illus. 50). The buildings, facing the street, house the mothers' living spaces, infant care, and common services, such as dining facilities and lounge space.[73]

The Mothers' House and the apartment building on the Quai de Jemmapes each accept the urban structure of their respective contexts by using infill building to strengthen the street wall. However, Van Eyck and Grumbach each respond to the ambiguous frontality of the courtyard building by expressing the internal life of their buildings on the street elevations. Thus the buildings achieve a somewhat object-like character because they reject the more traditional approach which shields the internal life of the building from the public life of the street and shows it, if at all, on the courtyard side. In the Quai de Jemmapes building, the large-scale expression of the community center, especially on the second floor (Illus. 51), reveals the semi-public nature of its program. In the Mothers' House, the brightly colored stair, indeed the transparency of the elevation, opens the housing itself to the street. The stair, the prime social center of the house, acts as a metaphorical entry courtyard, replacing any symbolic function lost by accepting the semi-private nature of the rear court. In form and function, it creates internal communal links between the homeless families, who share the facility, and external connections between the building and its neighboring community which the families will eventually rejoin.

The spectrum unfolds throughout the building because color and creating "enclosure by means of—or through—transparency"[74] currently interest Van Eyck. Internal transparencies, created by overlapping spaces in section and by using transparent materials, allow the changes in color to be easily perceived; Van Eyck argues that this helps encourage a greater sense of community among the residents. This is carried out brilliantly in the childrens' wing, where a skylit bridge connects the childrens' sleeping rooms and interior play spaces below to the adults' building (Illus. 52). This bridge also gives access to play yards in the garden and on roof decks. As much as the building encourages openness it does not deny the need for privacy. In the children's wing individual bedrooms sleep five

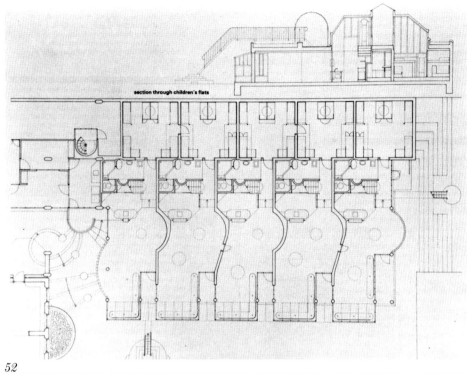

section through children's flats

52

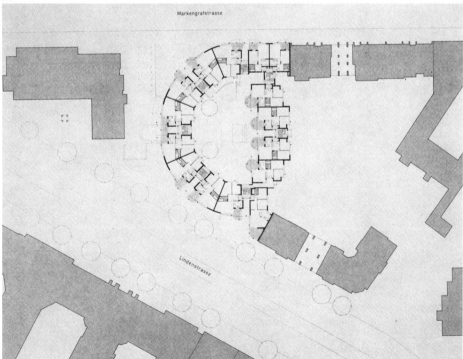

Markengrafstrasse

Lindenstrasse

53

52

Mothers' House, Amsterdam, The Netherlands. Aldo Van Eyck. 1974-1980. Section and plan of children's wing. Source: The Architectural Review 171 (March 1982), p. 32.

53
Apartment House, Berlin, West Germany. Herman Hertzberger. 1982-1986. Site plan. Source: NYSCA.

54
*Apartment House, Berlin, West Germany. Herman Hertzberger. 1982-1986. Photograph of courtyard. Source: Architect.*

54

children, the mothers each sleep in separate rooms in the main house, and the rear garden is reserved for the use of the residents.

The tension between the street and the court can also be seen in larger-scale courtyard projects. When such buildings occupy a city block or more they produce, unsurprisingly, more monumental internal courtyards than smaller-scale structures. The importance of these larger-scale perimeter blocks can rival that of the street since these buildings usually stress the courtyard as the residents' major public place with building entries often occuring off of them. In effect, the building turns its back to the street. Alternatively, the designs of several recent perimeter blocks have tried to mediate the courtyard's importance by manipulating its relation to other building elements.

In his housing project sponsored by the Internationale Bauausstellung (I.B.A.) in West Berlin (1982-86), Hertzberger takes advantage of the size of the infill lot to create a public space. Rather than differentiating the street and courtyard experiences, the project balances the importance of the two by treating them as more or less equal. Capping the end of an existing block of housing, the string of apartments bends to form the semi-circular perimeter which defers to a church at the corner of the site (Illus. 53). With each cluster of apartments grouped about an exterior stair, which Hertzberger characterizes as "vertical streets," the building massing breaks open to let the street space extend up through it and into the courtyard beyond. The majority of the units are entered directly from the street through the exterior stairs. These also provide tall gateways into the interior courtyard, where another set of similarly designed stairs provides entry for the units which face the courtyard (Illus. 54).[75]

This building draws on work Hertzberger designed in Kassel, West Germany (1979-1982), where the housing's massing also breaks open to reveal the vertical street of the internal stair, filled with light, air, and human activity. His Kassel project occupies two infill slots in a serpentine line of row housing in which different architects designed the individual buildings (Illus. 55).[76] In Hertzberger's two buildings the stair hall links two apartments on each of four floors (Illus. 56). The third-floor landing projects out from the building wall, creating a large semi-circular room which the residents use as a lounge (Illus. 57). Small entry vestibules, which function similarly to porches, overlook the stair, as do balconies and kitchen windows. This is intended to encourage neighborliness and social interaction.[77]

Hertzberger's Berlin project articulates circulation in the building and the courtyard to express housing as a collective experience. Thus his design emphasizes the courtyard more as a place of movement from street to building cluster than as a internally focused, placid space. The stair links the public space of the street and the courtyard with the private space of the apartment unit by spilling the semi-public space of the stair and balcony onto the building's elevations (Illus. 58). This design strategy superficially resembles that used by Colquhoun and Miller in the Hackney Housing in that the articulation of building circulation enlivens the housing cluster's expression (see illus. 43). However, unlike the Hackney project where the taut street wall separates the interior of the apartment from the street, the Berlin stair offers a series of projecting and receding terraces which physically engage the street and courtyard space. Fenestration, clustered near the stair and more continuous than the punched window openings of the Hackney project,

*55*
*Apartment House, Kassel, West Germany. Herman Hertzberger. 1979-1982. Site plan. Source: NYSCA.*

*56*
*Apartment House, Kassel, West Germany. Herman Hertzberger. 1979-1982. Cluster plan. Source: Archis (December 1986), p. 27.*

*57*
*Apartment House, Kassel, West Germany. Herman Hertzberger. 1979-1982. Section through public stair. Source: Architecture d'aujourd'hui 225 (February 1983), p. 63.*

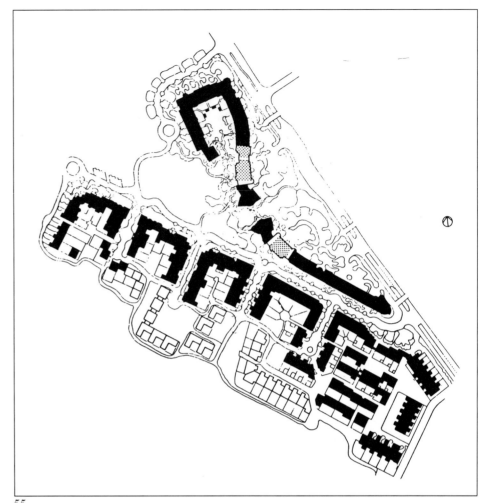

55

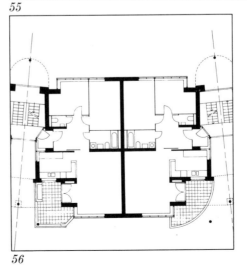

56

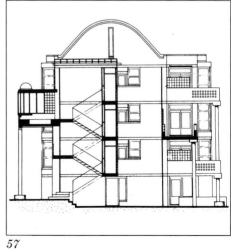

57

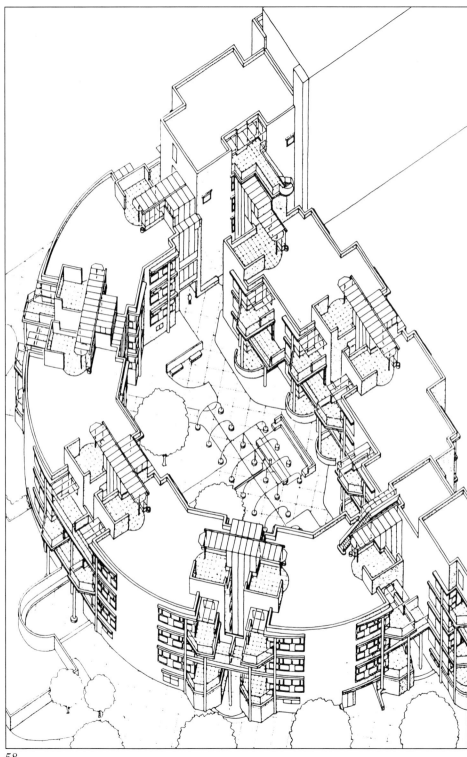

58
*Apartment House, Berlin, West Germany. Herman Hertzberger. 1982-1986. Building axonometric. Source: Architect.*

helps connect the apartments to each other and to the street. The highly articulated stair and entry sequence serves to architecturally define each cluster; maintaining the continuity of the facade's surface gives identity to the project as a whole, especially from the street side.

The design's exuberance does raise questions about the tenant's ability to maintain privacy; however, as Peter Buchanan points out in the *Architectural Review*,[78] the main entry doors to the units are solid; tenants can also add curtains to shield the kitchen windows and terrace doors that overlook the stair. In addition there are scale problems; for instance the three-story columns supporting the the terraces have ungainly proportions and appear, at times, to be unstable.

If Hertzberger blurs the distinction between street and court in his Berlin building by treating public circulation and fenestration similarly in both places, Bangert, Jansen, Scholtz, and Schultes do so by opening the massing of their Berlin perimeter block to the street, thereby defining the courtyard space with minimal architectural means. Also built by Internationale Bauausstellung (I.B.A.), this free-standing building consists of four, identical pavilions which form the corners of a raised, paved courtyard (Illus. 59). Double-story terraces, somewhat reminiscent of those Le Corbusier used in his multi-family housing proposals during the 1920's, connect the pavilions to each other and allow public view into the central paved courtyard space. Since this space is lifted off the street to create space for underground parking, stairs give public access to the court from which each pavilion is entered (Illus. 60). As in Hertzberger's Berlin and Kassel projects two apartment units occupy each floor; in this case two-story spaces extend the spaces of the terraces into the major living areas of the apartments.[79]

The Pentagon Housing, designed by Theo Bosch, is another freestanding courtyard apartment building that employs a design strategy similar to Hertzberger's. Located in the Nieuwmarkt area of Amsterdam it is part of a master plan of infill housing designed by Bosch and van Eyck in the 1970s. This master plan was developed because of community resistance to the government- sponsored transformation of the neighborhood into a business district served by a new subway line. Though the subway was built eventually, Bosch and van Eyck's plan kept the area's residential character, reconstructing the neighborhood fabric with select, careful positioning of infill housing and mews-like passages between blocks.

Bosch's Pentagon housing occupies one of the largest infill blocks in the Nieuwmarkt plan (Illus. 61). It is a small-scale, five-sided, perimeter block that borders two canals, a major street, and two mews. As in Hertzberger's Berlin project, the six-story concrete-frame building tries to balance the street and and courtyard experiences though Bosch sometimes uses different architectural means than Hertzberger. Thus, the building consists of a series of street-entered shops and apartments on the ground floor with flats and duplexes above (Illus. 62). These are entered from stairs that project into the courtyard space. The street facades, subtly modulated to meet the changing context, are similar to the courtyard elevations. Apartment terraces open to the street (Illus. 63) and are countered by the access galleries on the courtyard side from which the upper-level apartments are reached.[80]

In contrast, Edith Gerard's courtyard apartment house on the Quai de la Loire

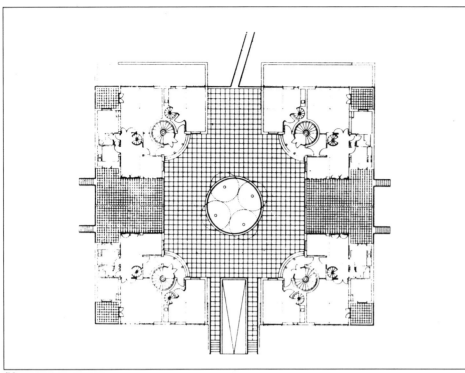

59

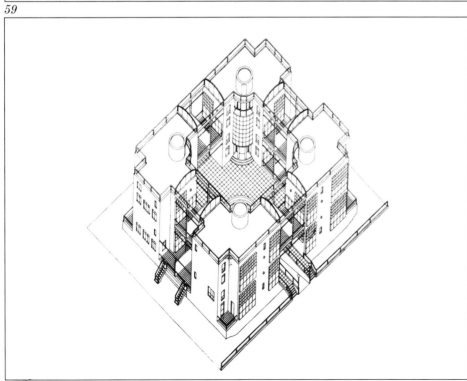

60

59
*Apartment House, Berlin, West Germany. D. Bangert, B. Jansen, St. Scholz, A. Schultes. 1984.*
*Site plan. Source: NYSCA.*

60
*Apartment House, Berlin, West Germany. D. Bangert, B. Jansen, St. Scholz, A. Schultes. 1984.*
*Building axonometric. Source:* Architecture d'aujourd'hui *234 (September 1984), p. 53.*

61
*Pentagon, Nieuwmarkt, Amsterdam,
The Netherlands. Theo Bosch. c. 1985.
Site plan. Source: NYSCA.*

62
*Pentagon, Nieuwmarkt, Amsterdam,
The Netherlands. Theo Bosch. c. 1985.
Ground floor plan. Source:* Architectural Review *177 (January 1985), p. 21;
or* Architectural Record *173 (Janaury
1985), p. 137.*

63
*Pentagon, Nieuwmarkt, Amsterdam,
The Netherlands. Theo Bosch. c. 1985.
Site axonometric. Source:* Architec-
tural Record *173 (January 1985), p. 139.*

62

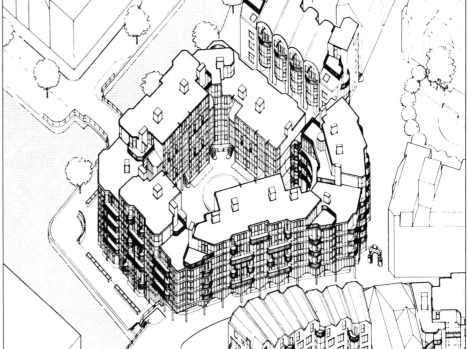

63

65

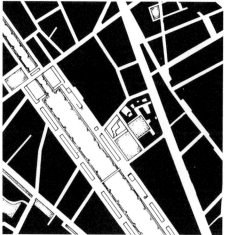

64
*Apartment House, Quai de la Loire, Paris, France. Edith Gerard. 1982-1984.*
*Site plan. Source: NYSCA.*

65
*Apartment House, Quai de la Loire, Paris, France. Edith Gerard. 1982-84.*
*Photograph of quai-side elevation. Source: Martine Cornier.*

*66*
*Mare et Cascades Housing, Paris,*
*France. Antoine Grumbach. 1983-1986.*
*Site axonometric. Source:* Lotus 41,
*p. 98.*

*67*
*Mare et Cascades Housing, Paris,*
*France. Antoine Grumbach. 1983-1986.*
*Site section. Source:* Lotus 41, p 98.

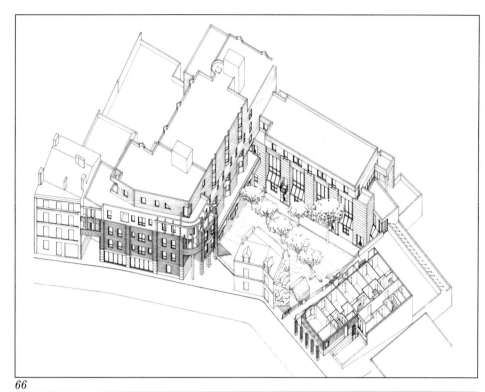

*66*

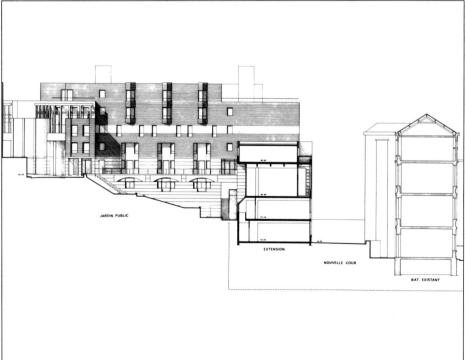

*67*

(1982-1984) in Paris works to establish differences between the courtyard and the street. Occupying a full, though small, city block (Illus. 64) along the Canal St. Martin, it takes advantage of the potential monumentality of this urban situation. Its elevations gesture out toward the city, especially toward the views along the canal, while the inner court remains a semi-private space. If anything, its outward facing prospect further privatizes the traditional relationship of public street and semi-private court found in most nineteenth- century Parisian apartment houses.

The scale and monumentality of the building's massing establishes a sense of place in a fabric composed of varying types of housing and public spaces. Split along the diagonal into two L-shaped buildings, the housing maintains its object-like character as it responds to the adjacent site conditions. The higher L along the Quai and the rue Dehayin consists mainly of flats which are designed to maximize views along the canal. Duplexes in the lower building face the adjacent park and housing. On the park facade, their larger-scale reading helps express the main entry into the courtyard, off of which the main lobby is located (Illus. 65).

As successful as the street massing and elevations are, the courtyard space suffers from ambiguous spatial definition. Given the prominence and scale of the street elevations, the courtyard remains a semi-private space. Gates prevent public movement through the courtyard; yet, the building entry is located off of it, and the diagonal separating the two buildings creates a visual slot that permits glimpses of the canal and the city from it. The courtyard elevations continue to shear the space. Although some terraces open onto it, for the most part, ribbon windows separate the life of the court from the life of the apartment.[81]

In the "Mare et Cascades" project (1983-1985) new low-income housing, workshops, and a school tie the complex to the existing formal and social context of eastern Paris. Like his strategy on the Quai des Jemmapes, here Grumbach "attempts to glue the bits together again,"[82] by leaving as many layers of history as possible open to public view. However, unlike Grumbach's Quai des Jemmapes or, for that matter, the Gerard building, the courtyard provides the symbolic center for the complex (Illus. 66). Required by law to preserve a medieval well on the site, the architect focuses his design around the central semi-public green space in which the well sits. This garden slopes down to meet the addition to the school with new housing closing both of its sides. Apartment entries, situated off of this space, assure movement through the space. At the top of the hill, the new housing and a renovated, yellow eighteenth-century house establish the plane of the street wall (Illus. 67). The house is freestanding and, the space between the buildings opens the courtyard's life to the street. A second, smaller paved courtyard serves as the entry space for a group of workshops. It sits further down the hill and is reached either by a driveway or by walking through the main space. The massing and elevations, in red and yellow brick, recall the expression of the city's public housing built during the 1920s and 1930s.

Grumbach's and other architects' use of traditional housing types, such as the row house and the courtyard apartment house, on infill sites has not fixed or limited the form of the European city; rather, based, as much of it is, on typological interpretation, it permits the continued evolution of the city and allows architectural invention. As the preceding discussion shows, the size of the infill site and the kind of housing are critical. Clearly, a larger infill site more easily permits depar-

*Ilot la Vierge, Elbeuf, France. Reichen
and Robert. 1985.
Site. Source: Architect.*

tures from the traditional relationship of the different housing types to the street than a smaller one does, as, for example, the Haarlemmer Houtuinen project in Amsterdam shows (see illus 45). By turning the interior of the block into a semi-public space this project challenges the traditional hierarchy of public and private spaces associated with row housing in a way that the smaller sites at the Hackney and Ashmill Street cannot permit (see illus. 38 and 40). In addition the relatively large-scale apartment house type permits much greater manipulation of building form than the row house, allowing the shaping of exterior spaces, such as court-yards, within the building's volume. Like the row house, it maintains the pattern of the urban fabric; its courtyards and other public and semi-public spaces can, however, more easily supplement the pattern. Thus as much Hertzberger's Amsterdam row housing articulates the experience of the inner street, the design of the courtyard and the entryways at his perimeter block in Berlin more fully modulates the city's public space (see illus. 58). The apartments in this building also benefit from facing both street and court.

In European cities rehabilitation improves substandard and dilapidated low-income housing ranging from medieval row houses and nineteenth-century tenements to mid-twentieth-century housing projects. As with new construction, this process occurs at the district, block, or building scale, and, depending on the form of building involved and the attitude of the designer, it either focuses attention on the street as public space or supplements it with other spatial sequences. Since restoration uses existing building it, perhaps more explicitly than new construction, faces the question of how best to adapt older buildings to meet the form of the contemporary city and its residents' social needs. When strict preservationist guidelines are followed the renovation meets (or mimics) exact historical standard. Rehabilitation can, however, permit the continued evolution of urban form through, for example, upgrading building standards and/or adaptively reusing of older structures.

Whether or not rehabilitation is accompanied by gentrification, the recycling of "substandard housing," such as the medieval row house or the nineteenth-century tenement, back into the housing market raises issues, especially when the renovation is used to house poor people. As in the United States, European urban renewal once destroyed much of the older housing stock now undergoing renovation because it lacked adequate plumbing, light, air, and open space. The original housing stock in, for example, the "Ilot la Vierge," Reichen and Robert's renovation of low-income housing in Elbeuf, France (Illus. 68) is similar to housing that many French cities once removed. Housing the poor in rehabilitated dwellings such as these can be seen as a way of stigmatizing low-income housing in much the same way as the anonymous and undifferentiated facades of public housing projects built in the 1950s and 1960s announced them as housing for the poor; i.e. the poor are no longer eligible for new construction; rather, they must inhabit older, lower-standard "slum" housing, albeit renovated. Demand, however, exists for this kind of housing, in part because of the failure of urban renewal projects to create adequate housing for both the poor and the middle class, in part because it provides amenities not found in newer construction.[83] Rather than limiting low-income housing to either newly constructed buildings or to renovated ones, a mix of both can be provided.

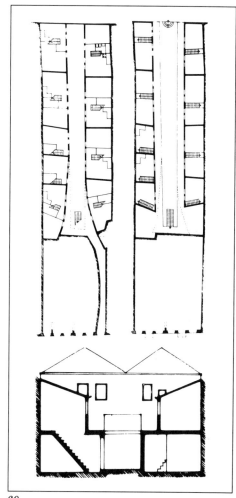

69
Rehabilitation proposal. Oporto, Portugal. Alvaro Siza. c. 1975.
Unit plans and building section before and after renovation. Source: Lotus 13 (December, 1976), p. 91.

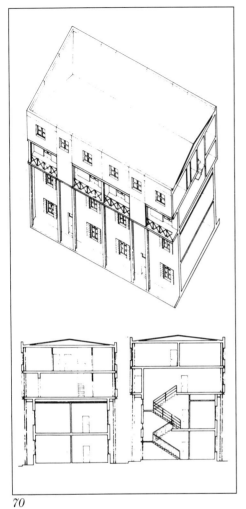

70

71

72

Balancing preservation with new construction is equally critical to the continued growth and development of the city. It may be appropriate on more monumental buildings to fix the form of a structure according to the esthetics of a particular period; certain historic districts may also deserve this kind of treatment. However, the rehabilitation of housing easily permits continued evolution and transformation of the urban fabric, especially when it is combined with new construction. As much as Reichen and Robert's project preserves the appearance of the original housing, additions to the building restructure its interior and its courtyard spaces. These, however, are masked by a stylistic uniformity between old and new. Other proposals celebrate the differences. For example, in Oporto, Portugal, Alvaro Siza has proposed using new construction on vacant lots, rehabilitation, and the reconstruction of buildings using existing foundations to improve the housing stock for various low-income neighborhoods in the city. His proposals for rehabilitation and reconstruction in the Sao Victor neighborhood respond to residents' expressed desires to transform the traditional "island" housing type and connect it more clearly to the street (Illus. 69).[84] Similarly, the participation of the Internationale Bauausstellung (I.B.A.) in the rehabilitation of the nineteenth-century fabric in the Kreuzberg area of Berlin mixes new construction with renovation. This project, also responding to tenant wishes, upgrades existing fabric, by adding new social spaces as well as new housing.[85]

If the renovation of older housing seeks to improve it by providing twentieth-century standards, the renovation of twentieth-century public housing projects seeks to add the amenities of historical building types and traditional urban experiences to newer construction. As in the United States, internal rehabilitation and more radical transformations involving demolition and the construction of new buildings create clearer sequences of public to private space in slab-block and tower-in-the-park projects. Renovation also repairs the physical problems caused by poor construction and building deterioration and adjusts the housing, often monotonous and institutional in character, to the needs of changing inhabitants.

In Cesena, Italy, the firm of Minardi Grossi has designed a two-story addition to an existing two-story slab of public housing (1982). Here, the architects define infill as increasing the population of the existing block in order to match the density of the surrounding context—now, the town's near suburbs. Charged with maintaining the original building, the architects extended its circulation system, where two walk-up apartments share a stair, into the new addition (Illus. 70). The architectural expression of the new addition gives a clearer front and back to the freestanding building. The upper levels, consisting of duplex apartments, sit on top of an independent steel frame that stands free of the original yellow stucco building (Illus. 71). This creates a shallow two-story arcade on the front and rear of the building. Slightly deeper at the front, the arcade becomes a large porch at grade, which opens onto stairs leading to upper level flats and duplexes; on the upper levels the frame holds terraces for the living floor of the duplex units. At the center of the building the terraces also occur on the fourth floor, marking the entry to the building's garden beyond, off of which entries to the ground-floor apartments are found.[86]

The renovation of Ronseray-Glonnires, a public housing project near Le Mans, France (1978-1980), by Douaire, Gulgonen, and Laisney, seeks to realize the potential of existing run-down housing. Accepting the immediate context of freestand-

70
*Housing Rehabilitation, Cesena, Italy.*
*Minardi-Grossi. 1982.*
*Building sections and axonometric.*
*Source:* Lotus *37, p. 63.*

71
*Housing Rehabilitation, Cesena, Italy.*
*Minardi-Grossi. 1982.*
*Photograph of facade. Source:* The Architectural Review *178 (October 1985), p.40.*

72
*Ronseray-Glonnires Rehabilitation, Le Mans, France. Douaire, Gulgonen, Laisney. 1978-80.*
*Photograph of renovated buildings. Source: Francois Laisney.*

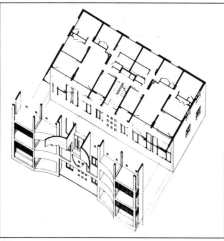

73
*Ronseray-Glonnires Rehabilitation,*
*Le Mans, France. Douaire, Gulgonen,*
*Laisney. 1978-80.*
*Axonometric and plan of apartment*
*cluster. Source: François Laisney.*

74
*Perseigne Rehabilitation, Alenon,*
*France. Lucien Kroll. 1978.*
*Site plan. Source:* Space and Society 6
*(September 1983), p. 39.*

75
*Perseigne Rehabilitation, Alenon,*
*France. Lucien Kroll. 1978.*
*Section/elevations through courtyard*
*before and after renovation. Source:*
Space and Society 6 *(September 1983),*
*pp. 38-39.*

76
*Perseigne Rehabilitation, Alenon,*
*France. Lucien Kroll. 1978.*
*Building axonometric. Source:* Space
and Society 6 *(September 1983), p. 40.*

ing, five-story, slab-block buildings surrounding large, irregularly shaped public spaces highly valued by tenants, the architects added new elements to the original buildings to strengthen their ties to the adjacent streets and public spaces (Illus. 72). Since tenant surveys and interviews identified the design of apartment units and entry sequences to the existing buildings as the major problems of the complex, the architects proposed increasing the depth of the original buildings in order to increase apartment sizes and to establish clearer entry sequences from the streets into the slabs and public spaces. For reasons of cost the renovation only improved the buildings themselves. No site improvements were included.

The work consists of a pre-fabricated system of parallel walls on both sides of the slab (Illus. 73). Those on the living-room side of the buildings form a continuous deep layer of space which enlarges the kitchens and terraces for the larger apartments. The terraces, originally recessed within the building mass, are now brought to its outermost plane, more strongly connecting the apartments to the street or court, depending on the building's orientation. This layer also houses new entry porticos, whose design adjusts to meet the street or the sloping courtyard. Its strong vertical orientation modulates the original building's low-slung horizontal expression by articulating entries and the different apartment clusters within the building. Since the residents did not identify the bedroom side of the buildings as containing major problems, their elevations were simply reclad.[87]

Lucien Kroll's rebuilding of "Perseigne," a public housing project near Alencon, France, seeks to tie this complex to the architectural and urban heritage of the neighboring community. Rather than simply repairing run-down housing, Kroll's design uses principles of infill building to transform public space in the complex and the architectural expression of its buildings. His proposal does not, however, completely mask the shape of the original *grands ensemble*; instead, it provides "points of attachment to the estate, which is after all an experience, an episode in the town's past."[88]

Brought to the project after internal protest racked the community during the mid 1970s, Kroll worked with the residents to develop a "counterlandscape" to the rationalism of the original project (Illus. 74). A new school, a community center, market square, parking, and streets were placed in newly designed courtyards surrounded by renovated slab blocks. The placement of these amenities, along a resuscitated path that once ran from town to the countryside, and the varied landscape designs for open space, which incorporate major sectional manipulations of the ground plane, give each of the previously banal public spaces specific identity and character (Illus. 75). They also allow the differentiation of the ground into public, semi-public, and semi-private outdoor zones. The architectural transformation of the slabs helps individualize the project (Illus. 76). The incorporation of ground-level additions, gable roofs, textured bricks, and other materials relieve the monotony of the original project; their placement also creates gates which mark entry into the site and strongly connects the buildings to the ground plane.[89]

Within the past decade the process of infill building has transformed low-income housing in western European central cities and suburbs. Whether produced by new construction or rehabilitation, many housing projects designed since the mid

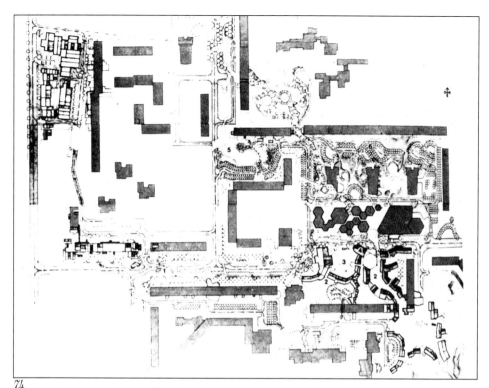

74

75

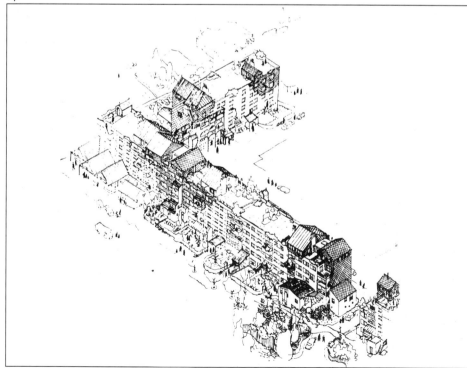

76

1970s reject the monotonous, institutional, and anti-urban character of the public housing projects built during the 1950s and 1960s. Instead, new infill projects, characterized by images which range from the monumental to the domestic, form public, semi-public, semi-private, and private interior and exterior spaces as they help re-establish the physical continuity of the urban fabric. Even the rehabilitation of post-war public housing has lessened its anonymous appearance. And, while budget constraints exist, low-income housing no longer necessarily proclaims itself "affordable" or "economical."

As much as the design of contemporary infill housing questions some aspects of the technological and functional determinism of the modern movement, it draws strength from other tenets of the modernist program. Certainly the historical importance of housing in modern movement reform proposals of the 1920s accounts, in part, for its central position in today's urban reform programs. The freedom with which contemporary designers interpret building types owes much to the modern movement's insistence on experimentation. Similarly, the current interest in flexible unit design and in making light, air, and open space available to residents parallels earlier work. The design of contemporary infill buildings also employs the benefits of technological sophistication, especially pre-fabrication and standardized building components, to produce more economical housing.

Unlike the open site proposals of the modern movement, the infill approach does not demand that a new plan govern the form of the modern city and its housing types. Rather new infill designs respond to the form of the existing city, its infrastructure, and its building types. They can resemble existing housing deeply, by using formal analogues of historical housing types, or superficially, by relying on stylistic imitation.[90] The typological approach to design permits new housing to be rooted in the history of the city, while also allowing it to establish connections to contemporary culture. Without compromising the experience of the larger urban whole, it leads to the creation of a culturally authentic urban environment, one which accepts both continuity and change.[91] It can also provide good, affordable, and, at its best, beautiful housing.

The typological approach to design accepts two strategies for designing infill housing in historic town centers: that which sees the block as group of individual buildings and that which sees the block the principle morphological element of the city. These approaches, rooted in the nineteenth- and early-twentieth-century housing reform movements, develop out of the sizes of available sites and respond to existing building typologies and urban morphologies. Each method offers different architectural and urbanistic advantages. That which sees the block as group of individual buildings, usually row houses, focuses attention on the public space of the street with the facade of each house representing individual households. This method is most useful for repairing small holes in the street wall with new or renovated buildings. The building type most commonly used to do this, the row house, provides a small-scale residential environment that speaks of single-family living, even though it may house more than one family. That which sees the block as the principle morphological urban element configures buildings for larger sites, usually with courtyard apartment houses, to provide spaces on the block interior which supplement the public space of the street. Since the apartment house is a more pliable type than the row house, it offers more choice in the design of apartment units, interior semi-public spaces, and exterior open spaces. Moreover the courtyard, bringing light, air, and open space into the interior of the block, physically symbolizes the greater numbers of people living in the apartment building as it mediates the public space of the street and the private space of the apartment unit. These two approaches are general design strategies; clearly room exists to interpret them, especially by combining different kinds of housing types, manipulating the sequences of public-to-private space normally associated with each housing type, and mixing new construction with rehabilitation.

Unfortunately, this last issue, whether to povide housing with new construction or with rehabilitation, has clouded discussion of the housing problem so much that the method of housing production has become a more important issue than the kind of urbanisitic and architectural attitude the housing displays. New construction is valued simply because it is new; rehabilitated housing is valued only because it saves old buildings. Both methods can create adequate housing and urban form. The choice, to a large extent, should depend on which method produces the best architecture for a given site rather than on trying to establish one process as inherently more valuable than the other.

The public sector subsidies of low- and moderate-income housing in Europe have enabled architects to test the theory of infill housing in practice during the past decade. Certainly American architects have examined some of the same questions and ideas as their European colleagues; many, in fact, have reached similar conclusions: infill construction is appropriate and desirable for low- and moderate-income housing in American cities. In this country it has been virtually impossible to implement these ideas, now well-tested in European practice, because of the Reagan administration's decision to cut public subsidy of low- and moderate-income housing and rely on the private market to provide affordable housing. Quite predictably this has not happened, creating a desperate situation for the working and non-working poor who now face daily the prospect of homelessness.[92] Affordable housing has become so scarce that any shelter, no matter of what quality, will do. As a homeless woman from New York states:

Years ago they built those projects, and this lady and her baby, they would have been put into a nice apartment in those projects. Do they build those places now? I read in the paper they are building something called mixed-income housing, and I studied it real close and what it said is that it's for the moderate, the middle, and the poor. The poor were people who had fifteen thousand dollars. I said to myself, "That isn't poor. That isn't no way near where I am at. What good will that do for somebody like me?" If they'd just fix up some of these places, boarded buildings, they're all over—they're *every* place you go in New York City—I would love it. It doesn't need to have a back yard. It doesn't need to have no pretty floor. It could be by dumpside city and it wouldn't bother me. Why don't they fix those buildings?[93]

Clearly low- and moderate income-housing should not have rats and broken windows, just as it should have apartments receiving adequate light and air, enough open space serving each apartment building or row house, and a form which shapes and symbolizes the public realm of our cities. Infill housing can satisfy these needs. But it can only do so, as the above plea for housing implies, when public financing of affordable housing exists once again in this country.

## Footnotes

The author would like to thank Martine Cornier, Karen Johnson, Debin Schliesman, and Catherine Teegarden for assistance with research and photography; Robin Auchincloss, Lizzette Lebron, and Francesca Moran for documenting and drawing site plans; the staff of Avery Library at Columbia University, especially Kate Chipman, for research assistance; and Eugene Sparling, for editorial advice.

1.
Antoine Grumbach, "The Art of Completing a City: Three Projects for Paris," *Lotus* 41 (January 1984), p. 96.
2.
Rachel G. Bratt, "Public Housing: The Controversy and Contribution," *Critical Perspectives in Housing*, ed. R.G. Bratt, C. Hartman, and A. Meyerson (Philadelphia, 1986), pp. 335, 345; Peter Marcuse, "Why Are There Homeless?" *The Nation* 224 (April 4, 1986), pp. 426-429.
3.
New York State Council on the Arts, *Inner City Infill: A Housing Competition for Harlem* (New York, 1985), pp. 17-18.
4.
Since 1984 there have been a number of housing competitions in the United States which have been based on the principle of infill building. In addition to the "Inner City Infill Competition," these have included "A New American House," for Minneapolis, Minnesota (1984); "Artists Live/Work Space," for Boston, Massachusetts (1986); "Vacant Lots," for New York, New York (1987); and "The Art of Downtown Housing," for Seattle, Washington (1988).
5.
Architects of the modern movement did design infill building, for example Le Corbusier's "Porte Molitor Apartments." However, the principle of infill building did not structure the theory of modern movement urbanism.

6.
See, for example, Aldo Rossi, *The Architecture of the City*, (Cambridge, Mass., 1982).
7.
Vittorio Gregotti's introduction to a discussion of Alvaro Siza's work in Porto comments on this issue. See *Lotus* 18 (March 1978), p. 64.
8.
Council on the Arts, *Inner City Infill*, pp. 22-41.
9.
Charles Lockwood, *Bricks and Brownstone* (New York, 1972), *passim*; Alfred Medioli, "Housing Form and Rehabilitation in New York City," *Housing Form and Public Policy in the United States*, ed. Richard Plunz (New York, 1980), pp. 134-9.
10.
Infill building defines a building process in the late twentieth century which seeks to replace missing "teeth" in the fabric of the city. The scale of this replacement process, as discussed above, can range from individual buildings and blocks to whole sections of neighborhoods; its form is, very often, inspired by the dense, continuous nineteenth century city fabric established by party-wall building.
11.
See, for instance, Ernest Flagg's advocacy of the new-law tenement in Mardges Bacon, *Ernest Flagg: Beaux-Arts Architect and Urban Reformer* (Cambridge, Mass., 1986), pp. 234-258; also Eugene Henard's proposals for Paris in his *Etudes sur les transformations de Paris* (Paris, 1982), pp. 24-51.
12.
*Tomorrow: A Peaceful Road to Real Reform* was first published in 1898; starting in 1902 the book was called *Garden Cities of Tomorrow*. Le Corbusier's *Urbanisme* was published in English as *The City of Tomorrow* in 1929, translated by Frederick T. Etchells.
13.
Ebenezer Howard, *Garden Cities of To-*

*morrow,* ed. F. J. Osborne (Cambridge, Mass., 1965), p. 152.

14.
Ulrich Conrads (ed.), *Programs and Manifestos on Twentieth Century Architecture* (Cambridge, Mass., 1975), pp. 137-145.

15.
Bernard Huet, "The City as Dwelling Space: Alternatives to the Charter of Athens," *Lotus* 41 (January 1984), pp. 6-17.

16.
Conrads, *Manifestos*, p. 143.

17.
Discussion of these themes runs throughout Catherine Bauer's *Modern Housing* (New York, 1934), see especially pp. 119-134, and Donald I. Grinberg, "Modernist Housing and Its Critics: The Dutch Contributions," *Harvard Architecture Review* I (Spring 1980), pp. 148-150.

18.
Bauer, *Modern Housing*, p. 61.

19.
For discussion of this subject in New York City see James Ford, *Slums and Housing* (New York, 1936), Anthony Jackson, *A Place Called Home* (Cambridge, Mass., 1976) and Richard Plunz, *Habiter New York* (Brussels, 1980); in Germany and France see Nicolas Bullock and James Read, *The Movement for Housing Reform in Germany and France* (Cambridge, 1985); in England see Enid Gauldie, *Cruel Habitations* (London, 1974) and John Nelson Tarn, *Five Percent Philanthropy* (London, 1973).

20.
For detailed discussion of this subject see Plunz, *Habiter New York* and Jackson, *A Place Called Home.*

21.
John Reps, *The Making of Urban America* (Princeton, New Jersey, 1965), pp. 296-299.

22.
Ford, *Slums*, pp. 122-204, 266; Jackson, *Home*, pp. 16-17, Plunz, *Habiter*, pp. 19-

21, Reps, *Making*, p. 299.

23.
Ford, *Slums*, pp. 164-5; Jackson, *Home*, pp. 61-2; Plunz, *Habiter*, pp. 33-6.

24.
Bacon, *Ernest Flagg*, pp. 234-258; Ernest Flagg, "The Planning of Apartment Houses and Tenements," *Architectural Review* 10 (1903), pp. 85-90; Plunz, *Habiter*, pp. 44-51. Flagg also designed a three-bay building shaped like a "U" and a two-bay building shaped like a "T." This latter type, which is entered directly from the street and does not have a semi-public courtyard, became the most commonly built form of the new law-tenement.

25.
Henry Roberts, *The Dwellings of the Laboring Classes* (London, 1853); Tarn, *Five Per Cent Philanthropy*, p. 20.

26.
White achieved these lower densities because he limited to five per cent the amount of profit he expected his investment to produce. See Plunz, *Habiter*, pp. 85-89; Alfred Treadway White, *Improved Dwellings for the Laboring Classes* (New York, 1879) and *The Riverside Buildings of the Improved Industrial Dwellings Company* (Brooklyn, 1890).

27.
For examples of perimeter projects see Marta Gutman and Richard Plunz, "The New York Ring," *Eupalino* l (1984), pp. 32-47; Plunz, *Habiter*, pp. 118-133; 141-148.

28.
"The Paul Laurence Dunbar Apartments New York City," Architecture 59 (January 1929), pp. 5-12.

29.
Talbot Hamlin, "New York Housing: Harlem River Houses and Williamsburg Houses," *Pencil Points* 19 (May 1938), pp. 281-92; New York City Housing Authority, *Toward the End To Be Achieved* (New York, 1937), pp. 11-12; Plunz, *Habiter*, p. 17l; James Sanders and Roy Strickland, "Harlem River

Houses, *Harvard Architecture Review* 2 (Spring 1981), pp. 48-59.
30.
New York City Housing Authority, *East River Houses* (New York, 1941); Plunz, *Habiter*, pp. 193-5.
31.
Jane Jacobs, *Death and Life of Great American Cities* (New York, 1961), *passim*, especially pp. 200-221; Oscar Newman, *Defensible Space* (New York, 1972), pp. 1-21. In 1968 New York City's Housing and Development Administration issued *Plans and People: Vest-Pocket Housing, the First Step in New York City's Model Cities Program.* This was one of the first city publications to support the construction of infill housing.
32.
For two different perspectives on this questions see Bratt, "Public Housing," *Critical Perspectives on Housing*, ed. Bratt, *etal.*, pp. 335-358 and Susan LaRosa, "The Evolution of the James Monroe Houses," *New York Affairs* 8 (September 1984), pp. 89-99.
33.
For discussion of the Smithsons see Peter Eisenman, "From Golden Lane to Robin Hood Gardens. . ." *Oppositions* l (September 1973), pp. 27-56 and Alison Smithson, (ed.) *Team 10 Primer* (London, 1965); for discussion of Davis, Brody and Associates see Stanley Abercrombie, "New York Housing Breaks the Mold," *Architecture Plus* l (November 1973), pp. 63-75; Peter Blake, "Riverbend Houses," *Architectural Forum* 13l (July/August 1969), pp. 46-55.
34.
Marie Christine Gangneux, "Derriere le miroir," *Architecture d'aujourd'hui* 186 (August/September 1976), pp. 1-14.
35.
Kenneth Frampton, "U.D.C.: Low Rise High Density Housing Prototype," *Architecture d'aujourd'hui* 186 (August/September 1976), pp. 15-21; "Low Rise, High Density," *Progressive Architecture* 54 (December 1973), pp. 56-63; Museum of Modern Art, *Another Chance for Housing: Low-rise Alternatives— Brownsville, Brooklyn, Fox Hills, Staten Island* (New York, 1973), pp. 13-72.
36.
"Mott-Haven Infill in the South Bronx," *Architectural Record* 160 (August 1976), pp. 114-116. For discussion of recent infill projects in New York, see Plunz, *Habiter* and the forthcoming English edition to be published by Columbia University Press in 1988.
37.
Medioli, "Housing Form and Rehabilitation," *Housing Form and Public Policy*, ed. Plunz, pp.129-157.
38.
For example one of the first laws regulating tenement design in New York (1867) required the renovation of existing tenements. It called for the addition of adequate fire escapes, suitable sanitary facilities, ventilated bathrooms and halls. See Jackson, *Home*, p. 32.
39.
Robert D. Kohn and Andrew A. Thomas, "Is It Advisable to Remodel Slum Tenements," *The Architectural Record* 48 (November 1920), pp.417-426; Medioli, "Housing Form and Rehabilitation," *Housing Form and Public Policy*, ed. Plunz, p. 129.
40.
The Housing Authority would have preferred to clear the site and build new housing from scratch; however subsidies received from the federal government required rehabilitation. See New York City Housing Authority, *First Houses* (New York, 1935), pp. 20-21, 24-28; Medioli, "Housing Form and Rehabilitation," *Housing Form and Public Policy*, ed. Plunz, pp. 142-3; Plunz, *Habiter*, p. 168.
41.
Margaret Knepper and George Stoney in "Henry Street Settlement Studies: Can We Renovate the Slums," (New York, January, 1939) conclude moderate rehabilitation is feasible.

42.
A.R.C.H., the Architects' Renewal Committee in Harlem, advocated considering rehabilitation as form of low-income infill housing. See its publication, *Housing in Central Harlem: The Potential for Rehabilitation and New Vest Pocket Housing* (New York, 1967); Mary Camerio, "Community Design Today," *Space and Society* 8 (September/December 1985), pp. 94-105; Robert Kolodny, *Self-Help in the Inner City* (New York, 1973); Robert Schur and Virginia Sherry, *The Neighborhood Housing Movement* (New York, 1977).
43.
This form of rehabilitation was quite popular in the mid-1970's. Several universities, among them Pratt Institute and City College of New York, formed community design centers which continue to provide technical assistance.
44.
Conrad Levenson, interview by author, September 1, 1987, New York, New York; John Lewis, "Manhattan Valley Fights for Life," *The Daily News*, 9 December 1979.
45.
Medioli, "Housing Form and Rehabilitation," *Housing Form and Public Policy*, ed. Plunz, pp. 145, 151-4.
46.
The Community Design Workshop, Ghislaine Hermanuz, Director, *A Housing Platform for Harlem* (New York, 1985).
47.
Seventy per cent require moderate rehabilitation and modernization; seven per cent require major rehabilitation. Thomas Fisher and Daralice D. Boles, "P/A Inquiry: Privatizing Public Housing," *Progressive Architecture* 67 (May 1986), pp. 92-93.
48.
Daniel Ocasio, Albert Smith, and Richard Plunz, "A Prospectus for the Taft and Mitchel Houses, New York City,"
*Housing Form and Public Policy*, ed. Plunz, pp. 201-232; Richard Plunz, "Transformation of the "Tower in the Park"—Projects for Taft and Mitchel Houses, New York," *Lotus* 24 (September 1979), pp.61-75.
49.
Fisher and Boles, *Progressive Architecture* 67, pp. 93-7.
50.
Antonio di Mambro, "Restoration or Liquidation? Two Experiments in Public Housing in Boston, Mass.," *Space and Society* 33 (March 1986), p. 9.
51.
Fisher and Boles, *Progressive Architecture* 67, pp.92-97; di Mambro, *Space and Society* 33, pp. 6-19.
52.
di Mambro, *Space and Society* 33, p. 17.
53.
Interestingly Michael Pyatok, an architect from Oakland, California and winner of the Inner City Infill competition, recently noted that the current administration is pushing to retain an institutional image for what little public housing it now constructs. Pyatok, "Non-Profit Housing in Oakland, California," Graduate School of Architecture, Planning, and Preservation, Columbia University, November 24, 1987.
54.
Daralice D. Boles, "P/A Inquiry: Affordable Housing," *Progressive Architecture* 68 (February 1987), pp. 86-91. Other articles on Andrew Square include Sarah Snyder, "The 'Mutt and Jeff' of Boston Housing," *The Boston Globe*, July 3, 1986, pp. 17, 19; "Union Builds Low-Cost Homes in Boston," *The New York Times*, August 28, 1986, p. C-5; David B. Wilson, "Bargain Houses—No Speculators Need Apply," *The Boston Globe*, November 24, 1985.
55.
Michael J. Crosbie, "Gentle Infill in a Genteel City," *Architecture* 74 (July 1985), pp.44-48; "NAHRO Presents Honor Awards for Excellence," *Journal*
*of Housing* 43 (January/February 1986), p.24.
56.
Donlyn Lyndon and Marvin Buchanan, "University Avenue Cooperative, Berkeley," *Space and Society* 22 (June 1983), pp. 24-37; Sally Woodbridge, "Community of Differences," *Progressive Architecture* 65 (July 1984), pp.74-77.
57.
Crosbie, *Architecture* 74, p. 45.
58.
It should be noted that the Thatcher government has disbanded the Greater London Council which used to sponsor much of the construction of subsidized housing in London. Its responsibilities have been distributed to local authorities; however these authorities have constucted much less housing than the Greater London Council because of cuts in subsidies.
59.
For examples of alternative methods see Norma Evenson, *Paris: A Century of Change* (New Haven, 1979) on the French new towns. Mildred Schmertz contrasts Rem Koolhaus's support for slab housing in a Dutch suburb with Theo Bosch's use of more traditionally defined low-rise prototypes on infill sites in inner cities in "Low-Income Housing: A Lesson from Amsterdam," *The Architectural Record* 173 (January 1985), p. 134.
60.
This distinction has historical roots. See M. J. Daunton, "Public Place and Private Space," *The Pursuit of Urban History*, ed. D. Fraser and A. Sutcliffe (London, 1983), pp. 212-233; Donald J. Olsen, *The City as A Work of Art* (New Haven, 1986), pp. 89-131.
61.
This position has been articulated by a generation of contemporary designers. See Rossi, *The Architecture of the City;* Ignasi de Sola Morales compares the modern movement's dependence on contrast with the historical town with

contemporary designers' use of analogy in "From Contrast to Analogy: Development in the Concept of Architectural Intervention," *Lotus* 46 (March 1985), pp. 37-45.

62.

Comparison with work in the United States on this count is difficult because so much more housing has been built in western Europe. Certainly among the work discussed in this article the European work takes a much more pro-modernist stance than that in the United States.

63.

Robert Adam, "Radiance of the Past: Revivalism in Context," *The Architects' Journal* 178 (16 November 1983), pp.60-94; "Colquhoun and Miller: Public Housing in Hackney, London, 1983," *Architectural Design Profile 53: Building and Rational Architecture*, Demetri Porphyrios, ed. (London, 1984), pp. 85-86; "Doppelstadtvillen in London-Hackney: Colquhoun and Miller," *Baumeister* 83 (February 1986), pp. 30-31.

64.

Dan Cruickshank, "Under Starter's Orders," *The Architects'Journal* 182 (2 October 1985), pp. 20-23.

65.

In Dixon's project the purchase of the land was not subsidized; in addition the housing is intended to be occupied by former tenants of public housing. This forced economies: for example, no kitchens were installed, no floors finished, and walls were not painted. Rather these were left for owners to install.

66.

See Grinberg, *Harvard Architecture Review* 1, pp. 146-159.

67.

Herman Hertzberger, "Houses and Streets Make Each Other," *Space and Society* 23 (September 1983), pp. 20-29; Arnulf Luchinger, *Herman Hertzberger: Buildings and Projects, 1959-1986* (Den Haag, 1987), pp. 244-257;

"New Amsterdam School," *The Architectural Review* 178 (January 1985), pp. 14-38; "Une rue-habitation Amsterdam," *Architecture d'aujourd'hui*, 225 (February 1983), pp. 56-61.

68.

See, for example, Manfredo Tafuri, *Vienna Rossa* (Milan, 1980).

69.

Joseph Paul Kleihues, "New Approaches to Life in the Inner City: The Row or the Block?", *Architectural Design Profile: Post War Berlin 25*, Doug Clelland, ed. (London, 1982), pp. 66-69. For general discussion of the Internationale Bauausstellung's (I.B.A.) program of new housing construction in Berlin see Marc Bedarida, "Berlin 1976-1986," *Bulletin d'Informations Architecturales* 99 (December 1985), pp. 6-19; Susan Doubilet, "IBA '84: Exhibition/Collection," *Progressive Architecture* 63 (January 1982), pp. 197-204; *Internationale Bauausstellung Berlin 1987: Beispiele einer neuen Architektur* (Frankfurt, 1986). Marc Bedarida, in "The Adventures of Urban Design: Bofill, Grumbach, and Zublena in Montparnasse," *Lotus* 51 (September 1986), pp. 59-77, contrasts the impact of Bofill's monumentual classicism on the Montparnasse fabric with the more humanely scaled approach of the other two architects.

70.

D.J. Olsen, *The Growth of Victorian London*, as cited in Daunton, "Public Place and Private Space," *The Pursuit of Urban History*, p. 220.

71.

Bertrand Lemoine, "The Architecture of the Housing in the Municipality of Paris," *Lotus* 41 (January 1984), pp. 120-127.

72.

Grumbach, *Lotus* 41, pp. 102-3.

73.

Peter Buchanan, "The Mothers' House," *The Architectural Review* 172 (March 1982), pp. 25-33; Susan Doubilet and Aldo Van Eyck, "Weaving Chaos into Order," *Progressive Architecture* 63 (March 1982), pp.74-79; Ivy France, "Hubertusvereniging: A Transition Point for Single Parents," *Women and Environments* 7 (Winter 1985), pp. 20-22; "Lumiere, couleurs, et transparence," *Architecture d'aujourd'hui* 217 (October 1981), pp. 72-79.

74.
Aldo van Eyck as quoted in Buchanan, *The Architectural Review* 172, p. 30.

75.
"Woningbouw IBA, West Berlin" *Archis* (December 1986), pp. 34-35; *Internationale Bauausstellung Berlin 1987: Projetubersicht* (Berlin 1987), pp. 176-177; Luchinger, *Hertzberger,* pp. 333-337.

76.
"Weissenhof Cassel," *Architecture d'aujourd'hui* 215, (June 1981), pp. 73-83.

77.
Peter Buchanan, "Kassel Lesson," *The Architectural Review* 178 (October 1985), pp. 43-45; "Hertzberger Kassel," *Architecture d'aujourd'hui* 225 (February 1983), pp. 62-63; Herman Hertzberger, "Housing, Kassel," *Space and Society* 23 (September 1983), pp. 30-33; Luchinger, *Hertzberger,* pp.258-270; "Woningbouw Documenta Urbana: Kassel, Bondsrepubliek, Duitsland," *Archis* (December 1986), pp.26-27.

78.
Buchanan, *The Architectural Review* 178, pp. 44.

79.
D. Bangert, B. Jansen, St. Scholz, A. Schultes, "Un Immeuble-Villas: Logements sur la Rauchstrasse, Berlin," *Architecture d' aujourd'hui* 234 (September 1984), pp. 53-55.

80.
*The Architectural Review* 178, pp. 18-20; Tracy Metz, "Nieuwmarkt: A Community Victory," *The Architectural Record* 173 (January 1985), pp. 134-136; Schmertz, *The Architectural Record* 173, pp. 134-142.

81.
Michel Bourdeau, "Edith Gerard Paris," *A.M.C.* 7 (March 1985), pp. 64-69; Alain Plissier, "Repres Contemporaines: Edith Girard: Logements quai de la Loire," *Techniques et Architecture* 358 (February-March 1985), pp. 132-144.

82.
Grumbach, *Lotus* 41, p. 97.

83.
The rehabilitation of such neighborhoods as the Marais in Paris or, for that matter, the Lower East Side in New York, has preserved the physical form of the districts by repairing the deteriorated housing stock, more or less, on a building-by-building basis. The resulting rise in property values has, however, transformed these traditionally working-class neighborhoods into upper middle-class enclaves.

84.
Alexandre Alves Costa, "Oporto: The S.A.A.L. Experience," *Lotus* 18 (March 1978), pp. 64-103; Bernard Huet, "Alvaro Siza, architetto 1954-79," in Alvaro Siza, *Poetic Profession* (Milan, 1986), p. 18l; Alvaro Siza y Vieira, "The Proletarian 'Island' as a Basic Element of Urban Tissue," *Lotus* 13 (December 1976), pp. 80-93.

85.
Hardt-Watherr Hamer, "Careful Renewal in Kreuzberg," *Space and Society* 31-32 (September-December 1985), pp. 79-83; Internationale Bauausstellung Berlin, *Step by Step: Careful Urban Renewal in Kreuzberg, Berlin* (Berlin, 1987); Heide Moldenhauer, "Designing With Tenants," *Space and Society* 31-32 (September-December 1985), pp. 83-86.

86.
"Building on Tradition," *The Architectural Review* 178 (October 1985), pp. 40-43; "Building Up: Council Houses," *Lotus* 37 (January 1983), pp. 61-66.

87.
P. Douaire, A. Gulgonen, and F. Laisney, "Rehabilitation du grand ensemble Ronseray-Glonnires au Mans," *A.M.C.* 52-53 (June-September 1980), pp. 88-92; "Trois conceptions nouvelles pour le grand ensemble de Ronseray-Glonnires," *Techniques et Architecture* 348 (June/July 1983), pp. 96-99.

88.
Lucien Kroll as quoted by Franco Zagari, "In Search of Diversity," *Space and Society* 23 (September 1983), p. 41.

89.
Anne Vernez Moudon, "Platting versus Planning: Housing at the Household Scale," *Landscape* 29 (January 1986), pp.30-38; Zagari, *Space and Society* 23, pp. 36-43.

90.
Morales, *Lotus* 46, pp. 37-46.

91.
For an excellent discussion of the typological approach to design see Alan Colquhoun, "Postmodernism and Structuralism: A Retrospective Glance," *Assemblage* 5 (February 1988), pp. 7-16.

92.
Marta Gutman, "Housing the Homeless," *Design Book Review,* forthcoming.

93.
Mrs. Harrington (pseud.) as quoted in Jonathan Kozol, "A Reporter at Large—The Homeless, Part I," *The New Yorker* 63 (January 25, 1988), p.75.

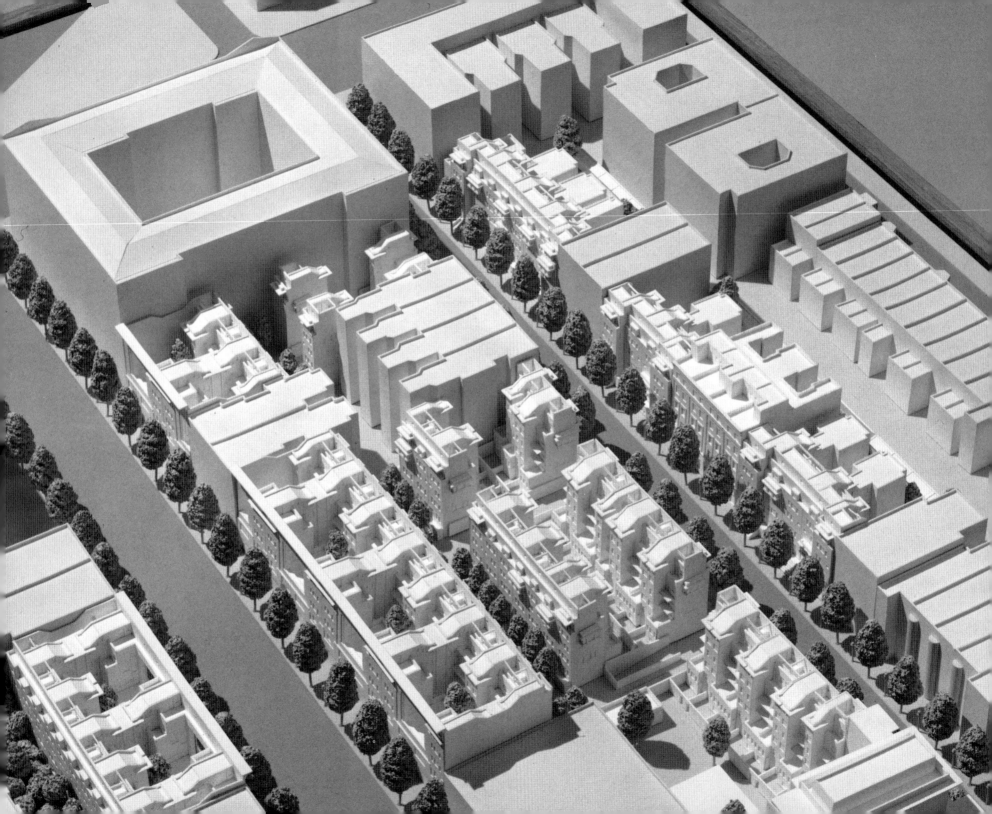

**Strange Fruit:
The Legacy of the Design
Competition in New York Housing**
*Richard Plunz*

*Stephen Campbell and Mark Nielson
Second Place: Inner-City Infill
Competition*

The architectural design competition has never occupied a place of great importance in architectural discourse in the United States. While there have been moments to the contrary (toward the end of the nineteenth century, for example), in general competitions have affected only a miniscule proportion of the total architectural patronage. By comparison, in Europe, the competition has emerged as a principal device for awarding commissions of all kinds, especially public work and social housing. In the United States the devices for selection of architects are less public, responding more to the exigencies of the private marketplace. Competitions for housing have been least frequent. The first was held in 1879, and it launched the critical period when New York came to be regarded as the American Metropolis. Since then, only eleven housing competitions in as many decades have been organized in New York City. Most New York competitions have occurred during a period of crisis in housing production, and have been tied to major reform efforts. Usually lurking beneath this equation has been the threat of social unrest as an outgrowth of poor living conditions. Within this pattern, the competition has frequently been used to reinforce reform efforts that have been too little and too late.[1]

The first New York competition in 1879 provides an archetypal case. It occured at the conclusion of a violent decade in United States history, focused primarily on labor rights. There were fears of even greater insurrection should the urban condition reignite the fuse. Housing conditions were a key catalyst. In New York, a practically uninhabitable housing stock had been newly constructed for the low income population, which was to say for well over one-half of the population. As early as 1865, a report stated that of a population of over 700,000 in New York City (not including Brooklyn, which remained a separate city until 1895) a total of 480,368 persons lived in 15,309 tenement houses of substandard condition. The most ubiquitous of this new housing was the "railroad flat," named after its plan organization which strung rooms from front to rear like a train, such that only two or four rooms out of sixteen or twenty received light and air from the exterior. This invention was the best that an uncontrolled marketplace in New York City offered. The housing competition held out the hope of providing relief from this growing affliction by generating alternative designs which could be equally profitable to the builder or landlord, and provide better conditions for the tenant. The competition demonstrated the feasibility of achieving both goals, but only the most profitable schemes were influential. Exposed was a dilemma which has remained an integral component of housing design reform efforts for the poor ever since, which was that within the political ideology of our market economy, housing reform can not be implemented without enhancing profits. And ultimately those profits must be paid for in one way or another by the same underclass who are supposedly the beneficiaries of reform.

The sponsor of the 1879 competition was the *The Plumber and Sanitary Engineer,* a trade journal and the voice of the burgeoning domestic plumbing industry, which had its eye on a potentially lucrative tenement market. The "railroad flat" usually had outdoor plumbing in the rear "yard," or in the cellar. The competition, however, required water closets and taps on each floor; an improvement for the inhabitants, and a source of expansion for the industry. There were other double edges as well. The winning schemes were those which offered the highest density of inhabitants, in order to meet builders' demands for maximum profitability. They also had to be built on single 25 foot by 100 foot lots, in keeping with the highly incremental development commonplace to the period.[2] These kinds of constraints virtually guaranteed continued substandard conditions for light and air. Compromise with quality was implicit in the whole conception of the competition. In itself, the requirement for systematic tenement prototypes to replace the less efficient ad hoc development up to that date could only be expected to lead to increased density with its consequent problems, and in effect, a toilet on every floor with a small airshaft had its price which was greater overcrowding and higher profits to the developer.

First place in the 1879 competition was given to James E. Ware's "dumbbell," with its narrow internal airshaft. (Illus. 1) The next three of the twelve placing entries had similar plans.[3] This outcome did not mean that other schemes from among the 190 entries did not incorporate greater use of light, air, and space. Many devised very ingenious ways to open up the buildings. (Illus. 2) These entries, however, were not sufficiently profitable, and given the overriding profit motive, use of the competition as a means of establishing upgraded standards was negated from the start. For this reason, the 1879 competition could only be seen as negative influence on standards, and was widely criticized at the time.

The Tenement House Act of 1879 (known as the "Old Law") followed the competition and legally enforced its results, providing the first substantial housing design control. On paper it set higher standards than the winning entries. But in fact the Board of Health enforced the lower level set by the competition winners and the Ware "dumbbell" became a prototype for tenement construction for the next two decades. This turn of events institutionalized the gap between the written law and its enforcement, a New York subtlety which has reappeared now and then ever since. By 1900 approximately 60,000 "dumbbell" tenements had been built under the provisions of the 1879 law. Rehabilitation to reasonable standards of this legacy still represents a serious problem in New York City today.

It was not until 1901 that the Old Law was revised to represent reasonable spatial standards for new tenement housing (the so-called "New Law"). Under the Old Law tenements could be built along airshafts only several feet wide, with the interior rooms opening on them. The most significant improvement offered by the New Law was an increase in the minimum size permitted for the airshafts, providing for a space akin to a courtyard. Two competitions preceeded the revision, but unlike the 1879 competition, their sponsors were public interest social welfare organizations. The first competition, in 1896, was sponsored by the Improved Housing Council;[4] the second in 1900 was sponsored by the Charity Organization Society.[5] The 1896 competition attracted nominal interest from architects in spite of an important two-day conference on social housing which preceded it. But the 28 entries were exhibited and did generate some public discussion. By contrast, however, the 1900 competition received 170 entries, perhaps due to increasing

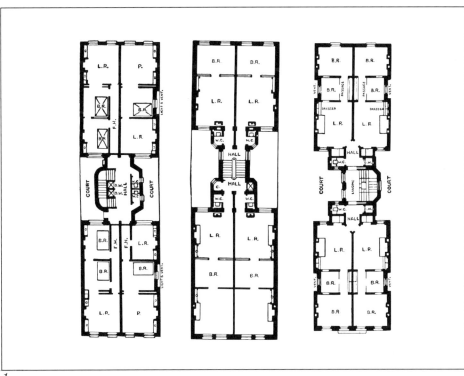

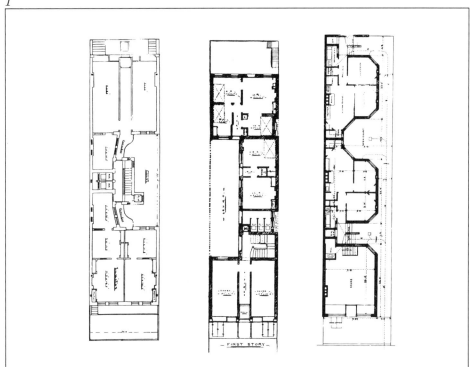

1
*First, Third, and Fourth Place submissions to the 1879 tenement house competition sponsored by* The Plumber and Sanitary Engineer: *Left to right: James E. Ware, Architect; D. & J. Jardine, Architects; William Kuhles, Architect*

2
*Sixth, Ninth and Eighth Place submissions to the 1879 tenement house competition. Left: George W. DaCuinha, Architect; Middle: James E. Ware, Architect; Right: Robert G. Kennedy, Architect.*

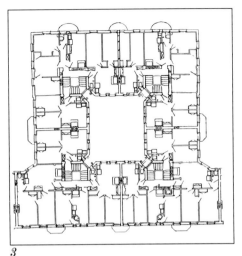

*3*
*First Place submission to the 1896 tenement house competition sponsored by the Improved Housing Council. Ernest Flagg, Architect.*

prospects for reform and commissions, and the promise of a major exhibition. The range of entries published from both competitions were more conservative than the wide variety of approaches published from the 1879 competition. On the other hand, the standards were much higher. The program required larger units with a toilet for each apartment. Rather than the single building lot, emphasis was focused on the block configuration. The use of a whole block meant that larger buildings could be planned around larger courtyard rather than airshafts. The units themselves could be bigger with more light and air reaching more rooms. This strategy could be traced to a seminal article published by Ernest Flagg in 1894 that outlined the logic of multiple lot planning.[6] The larger scale permitted economically practical solutions through the expanded design possibilities of multiple lot tenement organization, and proved that such plans could be attractive to the marketplace by creating better apartments at costs which could still permit generous profit.

It should come as no surprise that the entry submitted by Flagg took first place in the 1896 competition (Illus. 3) It incorporated Flagg's most generous variation, using four 25 foot lots. Central light courts provided public passage to the stairs for the upper floors.[7] James Ware, the winner for the 1879 competition took second place with a similar plan, which led to a public dispute with Flagg over the originality of the scheme.[8] (Illus. 4) Flagg's approach was an inevitable outcome of the practical conventions of tenement production in New York. The winner of the 1900 competition, R. Thomas Sport, used an identical massing approach.[8] The plan was reversed, however, so that the light-slots faced the street and served as the entry space. (Illus. 5) Flagg's studies and the two competitions facilitated the way for smooth transition in the tenement house law; the 1896 and 1900 competitions generated change in the tenement house law of significant and positive lasting value.

Not to be ignored in this important period of revision was the large housing exhibition held by the Charity Organization Society in February, 1900. It documented existing tenement conditions and showed the competition results. The scope of the exhibition has remained unmatched since. Other important efforts of the period included comprehensive housing studies such as the research by the Tenement House Committee of the New York State Legislature published in 1895; and another study published in the same year by Elgin R.L. Gould of the U.S. Department of Labor called *The Housing of the Working People*.[10] And by 1898, Flagg had completed a model tenement for the City and Surburban Homes Company on West 68th and 69th Streets, adapting his competition entry. In the following year he completed a similar project for the New York Fireproof Tenement Association on West 42nd Street. In 1900, Ware completed another for the City and Suburban Homes Company on First Avenue between East 64th and 65th Streets. The directed intensity of that particular moment has never been repeated.

Twenty years passed before the fourth and fifth competitions were organized, this time corresponding to the crisis in housing production created by a lack of building during the First World War and the brief period of stagnation which followed it. At that moment, New York City is said to have suffered the most severe housing shortage in its history. It was a volatile period politically, fueled by events in Russia in addition to the crisis at home. Again the threat of unrest created a climate for reform, and New York architects, more than at any other time, seemed to engage in these issues firsthand. An interesting barometer of the period was the

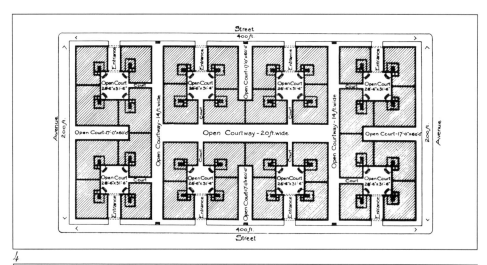

4

4
*Second Place submission to the 1896 tenement house competition. James E. Ware, Architect.*

5
*First Place submission to the 1900 tenement house competition sponsored by the Charity Organization Society. R. Thomas Short, Architect.*

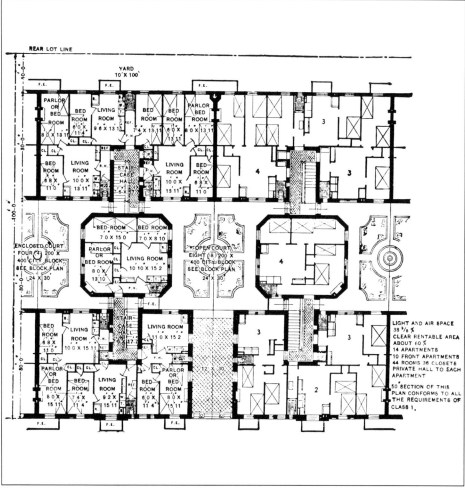

5

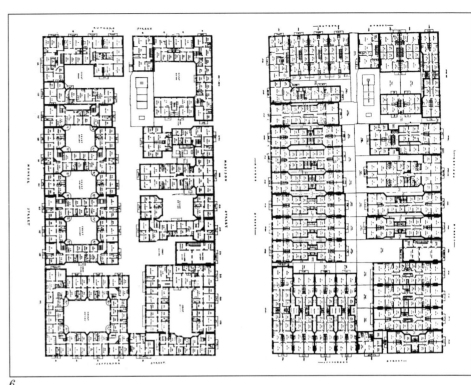

6

7

radical stance of the Housing Committee of the New York Chapter of the American Institute of Architects which advocated a complete government takeover of housing production in the United States. Another interesting consequence of the crisis was that for the first time the possibilities for rehabilitation were given serious consideration as an antidote to the shortage.

The fourth competition, in 1920, was for rehabilitation of a tenement block on the Lower East Side.[11] It was the only competition in New York City to focus on rehabilitation. It was also the first competition sponsored by a governmental body, the Joint Committee of the New York State Legislature on Housing and Reconstruction. The winning scheme by Sibley and Fetherston cut a series of eight courtyards into the pre-Law and Old Law buildings, in order to gain light and air.[12] (Illus. 6) While it improved existing conditions, new construction could have produced better design results. Rehabilitation was a controversial approach at that time, and the architectural discussion mirrored a larger political discourse. Many opposed the principle of trying to create acceptable housing standards from substandard buildings and thus; the debate on rehabilitation began and it has remained far from resolved to this day. By the 1920's, the minimum standards of the tenement era were becoming obsolete for new construction. The older tenement portion of the New York housing stock was relegated to the lowest level of the underclass, who remained below the reach of the reform efforts. New construction was moving toward standards affordable only to an emerging generation of upwardly mobile moderate income families. Within this context, Andrew Thomas, who served on the jury, argued that not only were the standards for rehabilitation lower than for new construction, but the process was more costly.[13] On the other side, those who supported rehabilitation argued that there was no choice in the matter; that the 50,000 remaining Old Law tenements were not going to disappear, and should therefore be improved by whatever means available. In time, the prosperity of the 1920's did produce an extraordinary amount of new moderate income housing. And the following five decades have produced little rehabilitation on the scale which this competition envisioned.

The fifth competition, held in 1922, was sponsored by a private philanthropic interest, the Phelps-Stokes Fund.[14] The program of the competition did not encourage innovation, asking for little more in terms of improved conditions than were already in place with the 1901 Tenement House Act. Required room sizes were increased slightly in recognition of the new market, but the program still reflected a mode of profit-taking associated with the earlier era of tenement construction. Winning entrants ended up tinkering with generous alternatives produced by the 1901 legislation, producing plans pretty much derivative of Flagg's ideas from three decades before. The first place submission by Sibley and Fetherston was simply a variation on housing which had already been constructed throughout the city.[15] More interesting was the Raymond Hood scheme which received honorable mention, but only Andrew Thomas managed to add some measure of distinction to the 1921 competition results. He ignored the program, tauntingly reducing the number of rooms per floor for a 100 by 100 foot lot from the required 46 to 42. This permitted the courtyard to be opened to both street and yard areas. (Illus. 7) But more important than this relatively minor improvement was an economic analysis of the Thomas plan made by Thomas and Frederick Ackerman.[16] They countered conventional wisdom by demonstrating that the reduction in rooms could actually increase profits, by decreasing initial construction costs and offering larger, more

*6*
*First Place submission to the 1920 competition for rehabilitation of a New York City block sponsored by the Joint Committee on Housing and Reconstruction of the New York State Legislature. Sibley and Fetherston, Architects. Inset shows a detail of the original fabric at upper right corner.*

*7*
*First Place submission to the 1922 tenement house competition sponsored by the Phelps-Stokes Fund. Sibley and Fetherston, Architects. Also shown is the disqualified submission by Andrew Thomas, Architect.*

desirable and more marketable apartments to a hungry moderate income constituency.

Although the winning design by Sibley and Fetherston was built on East 97th Street, the debate surrounding the Andrew Thomas scheme had greater impact. Unlike the competition program, his design rationale anticipated the changes in the economics and geography of housing production of the coming years that greatly increased minimum design standards for new construction. Larger units for moderate income families were available in the developing outer boroughs where land was cheaper than in Manhattan, and new public transit connections to Manhattan were in place as the New York subway system took its present form. These growth conditions were momentary, but lasted long enough to produce the remarkable new stock of housing. It was innovation generated by the marketplace, rather than by reform or by reformist competitions. Given the nature of the U.S. economic system, the marketplace, even with its vagaries, was likely to produce more innovation, however fleeting, than reform efforts. During the best of times, good results might be produced; but they hardly addressed the whole of the housing problem, and had little relevance for the poor.

In the 1930's, the marketplace euphoria was quickly decimated by the Great Depression. Predictably that economic crisis again spawned several competitions. They contrasted with the previous ones in several significant ways. For the first time with the New Deal came an impetus for direct government production of housing, with the hope of elevating housing for the poor from a formula-ridden morass of private development. While the previous competitions encouraged profitable challenges to the economics of traditional development in New York City, those of the 1930's did the opposite, with the assumption that government monies could overcome the problems of private production. Given subsidy, even in the highest density areas the acknowledgement of high real estate values and the need for high densities could be jettisoned. Suddenly the poor were exposed to the possibility of another world to which much of the moderate income population had already passed.

The new standards were reflected in the program for a sixth housing competition sponsored in 1933 by Phelps-Stokes Fund, which called for proposals for an entire block without specifying a minimum number of units. It encouraged design of a "small park" at the block interior, to be used by the general public and maintained by the city.[17] The kind of detailed technical requirements common to earlier competitions were dropped, in an effort to generate conceptual questions rather than technical answers. Incorporation of high-rise elevator buildings was encouraged for the first time, thrusting the housing competition into a realm which not many years earlier had been the exclusive domain of the upper class. The possibilities associated with higher building meant that the amount of ground level open space could be increased to a reasonable proportion of the total project coverage, without reducing densities. Given this liberalization of program constraints, the entries to the 1933 competition began to reflect present-day planning standards for the first time. The winning scheme by Richard Hutaff and Severin Stockmar defined the block in keeping with the perimeter block tradition, ringing it with a wall of housing. (Illus. 8). The typical New York perimeter block which tends to require a large central court due to the constraint of the grid dimensions was scaled down through internal subdivision. But the conventions of the traditional perime-

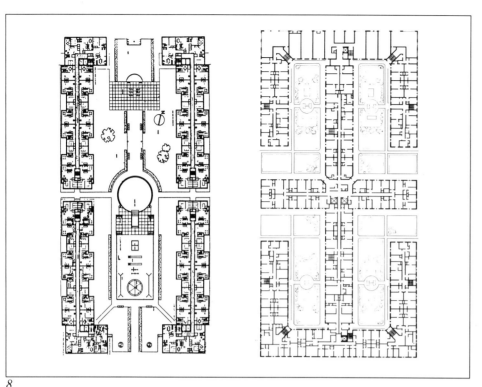

8

*Two First Place entries to the 1933
housing competition sponsored by the
Phelps-Stokes Fund. Above; General
category submission by Richard Hutaff
and Severin Stockmar, Architects; Submission to for the category incorporating a public park, William Platt,
Geoffrey Platt, and John M. Gates,
Architects.*

*9*
*Two placing entries to the 1934 housing competition sponsored by the New York City Housing Authority. Left: Horace Ginsbern, Architect; Right: John W. Ingle, Architect.*

*10*
*Site Plan for Williamsburg Houses as implemented. Richmond H. Shreve, in charge, with James F. Bly, Matthew W. Del Gaudio, Arthur C. Holden, William Lescaze, Senior Architects; Samuel Gardstein, Paul Trapani, G. Harmon Gurney, Henry Leslie Walker, and John W. Ingle, Jr., Associate Architects.*

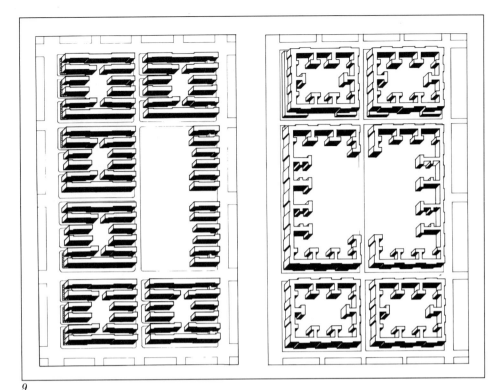

9

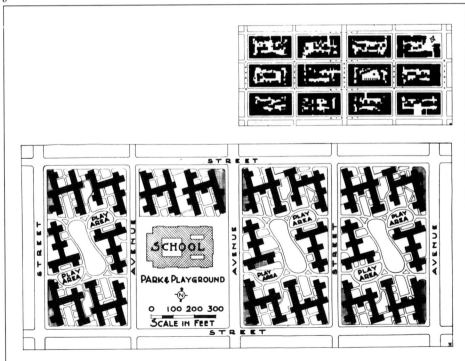

10

ter block planning were modified through division of the block into four smaller quadrangles.[18] A central cruciform elevator building was highest, surrounded by the lower exterior perimeter wall. Others of the competition entries were equally innovative. All of the surviving entries are variations on perimeter planning, drawing on the long tradition of the perimeter block, both in New York City and elsewhere, as one of the most successful prototypes for configuring urban housing.

In 1934 a seventh competition was organized by the New York City Housing Authority to qualify architects to design the new public housing of the era, beginning with the Harlem River Houses in Manhattan and the Williamsburg Houses in Brooklyn, the first Federally-supported housing projects in the city. It was the first government-sponsored housing competition. The program called for the redevelopment of a sixteen block area, using one of three possible population densities (100, 150 or 200 persons per acre). The permissable ground coverage would in turn depend on the density.[19] The competition site was one already assembled for the Williamsburg project, although it was somewhat simplified. Twenty-two architects were chosen from the 278 entries, and an exhibition of the work was sponsored by the New York Society of Architects. Because the competition sought to qualify professionals just as the government was about to embark on a major building program, the competition was more politicized than normal. The prospect of the massive new patronage would have been attractive enough in normal times, but it was underscored by the economic hardship of the Depression. There were well-publicized complaints from architects that the placing schemes failed to "represent the best in modern low-cost housing," and even that they were "illogical and....showed violations of the Multiple Dwelling Law." The professional qualifications of several of the winning architects were called into question.[20] But the most important questions came later when the time came to award the commissions for the new public housing.

The outcome of the NYCHA competition became interwoven with the changing aesthetic ideals of the era, which looked to the future and to a "modernism" which symbolized it, rather than the past and its traditional forms. In some quarters, the invention of modernist architecture was seen as an important expression of the potential of the culture to survive its latest crisis. What was loosely promoted as "International Style" modernism became intertwined with the expression of new economic and political power. Unfortunately for housing, the superficial application of this new "style" presented a threat to the reasoned body of theory which had evolved in the previous decades. For example, the established ideal of perimeter block planning, with multi-directional massing and courtyard gardens, was eclipsed by the modernist predilection for horizontal rows of housing, which was social barracks planning based primarily on the movement of the sun, rather than on cultural precedent. The breach between the two sensibilities was evident in the constant disagreement between the Housing Authority Technical Staff, who supported the established approach, and others who supported the new architecture. The latter included project architects as well as figures at the highest levels of power who were recasting the form and substance of the U.S. political economy.

In the face of the larger political and economic stakes, the competition of 1934 did not play the important role that had been expected of it in defining the parame-

*11*
*Placing Entry to the "House for Modern Living" competition sponsored by the General Electric Company in 1935. The drawing indicates use of 36 different electric appliances. Charles C. Porter, Architect.*

ters of the new social architecture. Most of the twenty-two placing schemes reflected the tradition which was in keeping with the sensibilities of the Housing Authority Technical Staff.[21] (Illus. 9). The critical Williamsburg commission, however, was placed in the hands of other architects whose interests lie with the new modernism. William Lescaze became the principal designer. He was an ardent proponent of the new architecture, and Williamsburg Houses became the seminal modernist social housing project in the United States. (Illus. 10). Lescaze was a member of the Housing Authority Architectural Board and had served on the jury for the 1934 competition, conditions which should have disqualified him from the commission. All of the four other senior architects for Williamsburg Houses also had questionable relationships to the competition. In the project that followed, the Housing Authority staff continued to propose perimeter block development and the outside project architects responded with "modernist" designs. The projects fueled controversy between the proponents of the new social look of modernism, and the advocates of ideas based on an understanding of social needs which had evolved over a half-century of housing reform. In spite of harsh critical reaction, Williamsburg Houses was the only New York housing project to be included in the Tenth Anniversary Exhibition at the Museum of Modern Art in 1939. Such was the force of design politics in the midst of economic disaster.

Although the era of the moderate income suburb did not begin in earnest until after the Second World War, its roots were set in place before. New Deal programs built the massive infrastructure of modern roadways, which was a key ingredient in realizing the transition to the detached single-family cottage as the dominent moderate-income house-type, together with its pursuant consumer culture. Already in the 1930's design competitions for single-family suburban homes were being sponsored by U.S Industry (General Electric, Johns-Manville, the American Gas Association, etc.), in collaboration with the new governmental agencies such as the Federal Housing Administration (Illus. 11). These events belied the planning which was under way to refocus the economy from the era of heavy industry to consumer goods. The design disciplines had to be aligned with this transition. In New York, for example, the architectural profession largely engaged an urban outlook, fostered by urban patronage within the context of urban culture. As well, for the common person living in the city, the small detached cottage was an anachronism. But the Depression shook this sensibility, having had its most devastating effect on the cities, and also on architects, reducing many of the best known professionals to a state of near-poverty. The record-level prizes for the cottage competitions were tempting and overshadowed anything offered for social housing. Most were national in focus, but with the eager participation of New York architects. The only such local initiative was a competition purposed in 1935 by the New York Chapter of the American Institute of Architects for an ideal low-cost single-family cottage.[22] It appears never to have been implemented.

Three decades intervened before the next housing competition was organized in New York in 1963. This long pause reflected the focus on the suburbs, reflecting the predominent values of the period. Ideas about urban housing were dominated by the "tower-in-the-park," a mixture of high densities with large-scale open space, which in some ways emulated the densities with large-scale open space, which in some ways emulated the suburban outlook. By the early 1960's, the general prosperity, combined with the Kennedy-era's emphasis on social reform, generated new money and new thinking about low and middle income housing. The

12

12
*First Place submission to the 1963 East River housing competition sponsored by the Ruberoid Company. Hodne Associates, Architects.*

13
*Second Place submission to the 1963 housing competition Edwin Stromsten, Ricardo Scofidio, Felix Martorano, Architects.*

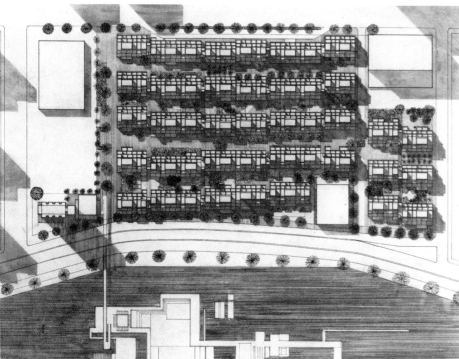

13

14a,b,c
*First, Second, and Third place submissions to the Brighton Beach housing competition sponsored by the New York City Housing and Development Administration. Upper: Wells/Koetter, Architects; Middle: Scofidio and Stromsten and Berman and Roberts; Lower: Venturi and Rauch.*

end of Robert Moses' domination of housing policy in New York City in 1961 helped encourage new attitudes, further nourished by the Lindsay administration's programs which reorganized the housing bureaucracy and encouraged innovation. The "bulldozer" approach to urban renewal was under increasing attack, reinforced by new theory centered around such figures as Jane Jacobs, whose influential book, *The Death and Life of Great American Cities* was first published in 1961. She argued for a return to a fine-grain and functionally diverse urban fabric. Serge Chermayeff, who with Christopher Alexander had published *Community and Privacy* in 1963, posed certain parallel arguments which pointed toward a reconsideration of the merits of low-rise housing types. In 1963, the program of the eighth New York City housing competition followed this new thinking, responding to the liberating effect of the recent reforms and the prospect of the new social spending. It set the standards for the unfolding discourse in the design of social housing of the 1960's.

The 1963 competition was the fifth in a series sponsored by The Ruberoid Company, a building products manufacturer, and was the first to deal with housing. It was also well-publicized and unusually well-funded, with $25,000 in prizes and the possibility of building the winning project. While the program assumed a subdized development, the spatial standards and community amenities were far higher than for the public housing of the period, reflecting the shift of subsidy into the realm of middle income housing in New York. The program was developed in coordination with the New York City Housing and Development Board, focusing on a four-block renewal area in East Harlem along the East River. The 1,500 apartments could take any high- or low-rise configuration, in compliance with zoning and building codes. Commercial space and parking was integrated, and special attention was focused on outdoor play areas.[23]

The submissions were diverse, covering a range of approaches and the jury was careful to reinforce new ideas. The winning scheme, by Hodne Associates subdivided the blocks into a small-scale gridiron of walkways and streets, which extended from the existing streets of East Harlem.[24] Four towers lined the water edge. (Illus. 12). This approach attempted to integrate the new construction with its low-rise context, and underscored the emerging importance of "contextualism" as a foil to the large-scale operations of urban renewal that had rebuilt entire areas with towers. After a number of years and many revisions, the same architects completed the project, and it ranks among the best of the new housing of that era. For this alone, the competition was unusually successful. The notion of combining high- and low-rise construction within a configuration of continuous massing became a common approach for the new social housing of the decade.

A more radical approach to the Ruberoid Competition was the second place submission designed by Edwin Stromston, Ricardo Scofidio, and Felix Martorano. (Illus. 13). It proposed a fine-grain, low-rise massing with narrow streets and automobile access limited to the periphery. This approach reflected the growing reaction against large-scale high-rise development. Given the strength of this resistance, it is surprising that more submissions did not reflect the same degree of questioning; perhaps witness to the attraction which the "tower-in-the-park" ideal continued to hold for the mainstream profession even by then. The scheme remains relevant today. In 1968, the ninth competition provided another opportunity for the same team to depart from the norms of the period.

14a

14c

14b

**15**
*Two placing submissions to the 1975
Roosevelt Island housing competition
sponsored by the New York State Urban
Development Corporation. Upper:
Stern and Hagmann, Architects;
Lower: Sam Davis/ELS Design Group.*

**16**
*Unplaced submission to the 1975 hous-
ing competition sponsored by the New
York State Urban Development Corpo-
ration. O.M. Ungers with K.L. Dietzsch,
Jeff Clark, and Arthur Ovaska.*

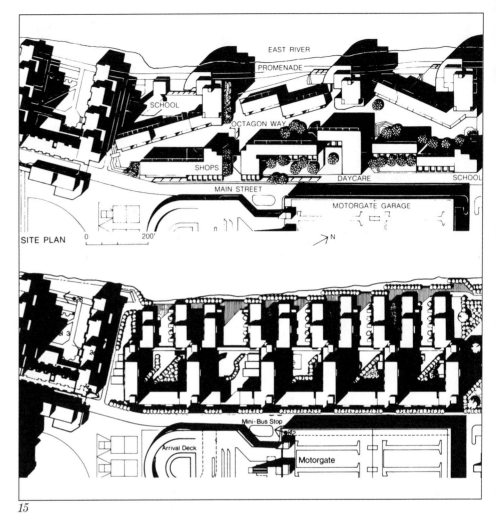

15

The 1968 competition was organized through the New York City Housing and Development Administration, with prize money donated from anonymous sources. It came at the culmination of a period of extreme urban unrest, which contributed to a sense of urgency regarding its outcome. The site, a stretch of oceanfront at Brighton Beach in Brooklyn, was to be developed for "moderate-income, limited-profit" housing along the lines that the State-sponsored Mitchell-Lama program had been building for some years. More importantly, it also reflected the emerging priorities of the New York State Urban Development Corporation which was launching a major building program for subsidized moderate income housing.[25] The winning scheme, by Wells/Koetter fit well into the upscale social housing of the period, with a twenty-five storey tower and six- and eight-storey buildings surrounding a public plaza facing the water.[26] (Illus. 14). The team of Scofidio and Stromsten, joined with Berman, Roberts, placed second with a radically different approach: a series of six buildings stepping down toward the water from eight to two storeys, with an intricate configuration of roof-top terraces. Although not quite as fine-grain as their previous experiment, the scheme indicated the same challenge of constructing a low-scale, non-monumental infill.

In spite of the potential of this latter scheme, most public attention was focused on the third place project, submitted by Venturi and Rauch. This emphasis reflected the growing influence of Venturi's ideas, especially of *Complexity and Contradiction in Architecture* which had been published in 1966. Two-storey townhouses were interspersed among two large thirteen-storey brick boxes which the designers argued were contextual in that they were evocative of the surrounding builder vernacular. This strategy was admired by some jury members as a sophisticated application of "existing possibilities." Others were critical, arguing "...that the buildings looked like the most ordinary apartment construction built all over Queens and Brooklyn since the Depression, that the placing of the blocks was ordinary and dull."[27] It was the first time in New York that "ugly and ordinary" were argued to be virtues for social housing; or that in general, aesthetic theory at the level of cultural nihilism was considered germain to the issue of design quality in housing. Yet the design quality of most social housing projects of the era remained problemmatic. Before all else, the issue of quality was tied to the political and economic values of the culture at large, making Venturi's polemic an indirect critique of the status quo, even if unintended.

In 1975 the tenth competition was organized by the New York State Urban Development Corporation (UDC) which had been one of the most important of the various agencies which had built the new housing of the previous decade. By this time, however, the period of large-scale social housing construction had already come to a close, forced by the first wave of Federal cutbacks and by New York City's "fiscal crisis." UDC was already in financial and political trouble and its large-scale housing programs were being terminated. UDC's demise coincided with New York City's problems, and with the crises of state which were focused on the Viet Nam war and on the Nixon administration Watergate scandal. The competition program called for the addition of 1,000 apartments to an existing UDC project on Roosevelt Island in the East River.[28] It tried to further develop the programmatic concerns of the Ruberoid Competition, focused on "community, child supervision, security, maintenance, livability, and responsiveness to context." With Roosevelt Island, social housing had moved definitively from moderate to middle incomes. The winning schemes remained unbuilt. The three placing submissions by Robert

*16*

Amico and Robert Brandon, Sam Davis/ELS Design Group, and Robert A.M. Stern and John S. Hagmann, owed much to the development of the previous decade.[29] (Illus. 15).

In other ways the UDC competition did mirror changing times. Historically, housing competitions had remained more the province of architects out of the mainstream; "housing architects" whose interests were stereotyped as concern for "social welfare" rather than "aesthetics." In this instance, however, the boundaries of this classic divide within the profession were crossed; perhaps partially due to the previous success of the UDC programs, which had hired well-known architects who received abundant publicity. As well, the aura of the 1960's with its "social involvement" was still fashionable. The UDC Competition was also unique in that the submissions included projects which were clearly visionary and polemical. In evidence was a curious mixture of modes, reflecting the growing turbulence in architectural thought and professional strategy. (Illus. 16).

By 1985, with the eleventh and final competition differing concerns appeared. In some ways it reflected the political concerns of the 1960's, perhaps affirming the critical importance of that decade in the formulation of the period to come. With the choice of a site in central Harlem, and with the development of a program placing particular emphasis on the cultural needs of a low income constituency, the program moved competition discourse closer than previously toward exploration of direct design responses to social imperatives.[30] The entrants were primarily outside of the media mainstream, and not heavily commercial. "Contextualism" continued to be important, focused on reconstruction of existing community fabric. In spite of this emphasis, the competition results could not conceal fundamental dilemas endemic to housing production. The outlook of the program and its submissions could not help but be overshadowed by the diminished resources for building housing for poverty level families; at a time when by official estimate, the population of New York City considered poverty level constitutes fully one quarter of the total, and has increased by ten percent since 1970.

The ideology of "home ownership" for the deserving poor has dominated housing philanthropy in the United States for over a century. It is a particularly strong ideal at the present, even if resources dictate the equivalent of nineteenth century mill housing in the center of Harlem, surrounded by the tenement shells which are being rehabilitated by the new urban professional class. The large question is whether or not this combination signals the beginning or end of an era. An endemic affliction of the previous competitions has been a certain disjuncture between architectural results and the political means. Those which produced the most innovative design propositions occurred in a context which lacked the possibility of realization. Those which occured in expansionist periods for housing produced design results which were compromised by the very prospect of realization. While this exercise falls in the former category, it has an interesting mix of both conditions. In a sense, it is an expression of continuity, frought with the collective frustration of its ten predecessors, strange fruit indeed in the Eden of the New York development world.

## Footnotes

1.
For additional discussion of much of the material found in this essay see: Richard Plunz, *Habiter New York, La Forme Institutionalisée de l'Habitat New Yorkais, 1850-1950* (Brussels, 1982). Revised English language edition published by Columbia University Press, 1988. An excellent general sourcebook for New York City housing competitions is: James Ford, *Slums and Housing* 2 Vols. (Cambridge, Mass., 1936).

2.
The competition program was announced in: "Improved Homes for Workingmen," *Plumber and Sanitary Engineer* 2 (December, 1878), pp. 1, 32.

3.
Plans of the first twelve winning schemes were published in *Plumber and Sanitary Engineer* 2 (March, 1879), pp. 103-106; (April, 1879), pp. 131-132; (May, 1879), pp. 158-159; (June 1, 1879), p. 180; (June 15, 1879), p. 212; and (July 1, 1879), p.230; "Prize Designs for a Tenement House," *The American Architect and Building News* (March 22, 1879), Plate 169. Contemporary criticism of the competition included: "The Tenement House Competition. Criticism of the Prize Plans," *The New York Tribune*, March 7, 1879, p. 1; "Prize Tenements," *The New York Times*, March 16, 1879, p.6; Alfred J. Bloor, "Suggestions for a Better Method of Building Tenant-Houses in New York," *American Architect and Building News* (February 12, 1881), p.75;

4.
The competition program was announced in Improved Housing Council, *Conditions of Competition for Plans of Model Apartment Houses* (New York, 1896).;

5.
The competition program was announced in: The Tenement House Committee of the Charity Organization Society, *Competition for Plans of Model Tenements* (New York, 1899).;

6.
Ernest Flagg, "The Tenement-House Evil and Its Cure," *Scribner's Magazine* 16 (July, 1894), pp. 108-117.;

7.
Notice and contemporary criticism of the winning schemes were published in: "New York's Great Movement for Housing Reform," *Review of Reviews* 14 (December, 1896), pp. 692-701; "Model Apartment Houses," *Architecture and Building* 26 (January 2, 1897), pp. 7-10. Also see Robert DeForest and Lawrence Veiller, *The Tenement House Problem* (New York, 1903), pp. 107-109; Ford, *Slums and Housing*, Plate 7; Anthony Jackson, *A Place Called Home. A History of Low-Cost Housing in Manhattan* Cambridge, Mass., 1976), pp. 106-108.;

8.
"Plans For Model Tenements," *New York Times* (June 3, 1896), p. 8; "The Housing Council Plans," *New York Daily Tribune* (June 11, 1896), p. 12.;

9.
Notice and contemporary criticism of the winning schemes were published in: "The Charity Organization Society's Tenement House Competition," *The American Architect and Building News* 67 (March 10, 1900), pp. 77-79; "The Model Tenement House Competition," *Architecture* 1 (March 15, 1900), pp. 104-105; "Model Tenement Floors," *Real Estate Record and Builders' Guide* 65 (March 17, 1900), pp. 452-455. Also see DeForest and Veiller, *Op. Cit.*, pp. 109-113; Ford, *Op. Cit.*, Plates 8, 9.;

10.
New York State Assembly, Tenement House Committee, *Report of 1894*, New York State Legislative Document No. 37 (Albany, January, 1895); Elgin R. L. Gould, *The Housing of the Working People: Eighth Special Report of the Commissioner of Labor* (Washington, D.C.: U.S. Government Printing Office, 1895).;

11.
The competition program is found in New York State Legislative Committee on Housing and the Reconstruction Commission of the State of New York, *Housing Conditions: Program of Architectural Competition for the Remodeling of a New York City Tenement Block* New York State Legislative Document No. 78 (1920).;

12.
Notice and contemporary criticism of the winning schemes were published in "Architectural Competition for the Remodeling of a New York City Tenement Block," *Journal of the American Institute of Architects* (May, 1920), pp. 198-199; "Notes of an Architectural Competition for Remodeling of a Tenement Block," *The American Architect* 118 (September 8, 1920), pp. 305-314; Andrew Thomas and Robert D. Kohn; "Is It Advisable to Remodel Slum Tenements?" *The Architectural Record* 48 (November, 1920), pp. 417-426.;

13.
Thomas and Kohn, "Is It Advisable.";

14.
The original program announcement is no longer extant. It was republished in Ford, *Slums and Housing*, pp. 915-918.;

15.
Notice and contemporary criticism of the winning schemes were published in: "Awards Announced in Tenement Plan Competition," *Real Estate Record and Builders' Guide* 109 (Februrary 11, 1922), p. 182; "Tenement House Planning," *The Architectural Forum* 36 (April, 1922), pp. 157-159; Frederick L. Ackerman, "The Phelps-Stokes Fund Tenement House Competition," *Journal of the American Institute of Architects* 10 (March, 1922), pp. 76-82. Also see Ford, *Slums and Housing* Plate 17. Considerable material related to the competition is found in the I. N. Phelps-Stokes Papers, New York Historical Society. Box 12 and Letter Press Book No. 17.;

16.
Ackerman, "The Phelps-Stokes Fund Tenement House Competition."

17.
The competition program was announced in an untitled pamphlet in the Phelps-Stokes Collection, Schomberg Center for Research in Black Culture, New York Public Library. Box 9, A-50 to A-75. The collection contains other material on the competition.
18.
Notice and contemporary criticism of the winning schemes were published in "Garden Space Stressed in Low Cost Housing Design," *Real Estate Record and Builders' Guide* 131 (June 3, 1933). Also Ford, Plate 22.
19.
The competition program is found in New York City Housing Authority, *Program of Competition for Qualification of Architects* (New York, June 18, 1934). The Fiorello H. LaGuardia Archives, LaGuardia Community College. Box II, 15A4, Folder 64. The collection contains other material on the competition.
20.
"Prize Plans Held 'Illogical' Housing," *New York Times* (September 8, 1934), p. 17.
21.
Notice and contemporary criticism of the winning schemes were published in "Selecting N.Y. Housers," *Architectural Forum* 60 (May, 1934), p. 27; "Selected Housers," *Architectural Forum* 61 (September, 1934), p. 5; "Drawings Exhibited For Low-Cost Housing," *New York Times* (September 5, 1934), p. 23. The placing schemes are found in: New York City Housing Authority, *Competition: Scrapbook of Placing Entries* (1934). A portfolio of the competition drawings in the Avery Architectural and Fine Arts Library, Columbia University.
22.
"Low Cost Housing. New York Chapter Competition," *The Octagon. A Journal of the American Institute of Architects* 7 (March, 1935), pp. 15-16.
23.
The competition program is found in

The Ruberoid Company, *Fifth Annual Architectural Design Competition, East River Urban Renewal Project* (New York, 1963), pp. 4-7
24.
Notice and contemporary criticism of the winning schemes were published in The Ruberoid Company, *Fifth Annual* "25,000 Ruberoid Competition Uses Manhattan Urban Renewal Project," *Architectural Record* 133 (February, 1963), p.23; "Renewal Gains From Ruberoid Contest," *Architectural Forum* 119 (September, 1963), p. 7; "Ruberoid Award Winners Announced," *Architectural Record* 139 (September, 1963), p. 10; "Minneapolitans Win Ruberoid Competition," *Progressive Architecture* 34 (September, 1963), pp. 65-66; "Ruberoid Competition Gives New York Ideas For Urban Renewal," *Architectural Record* 139 (October, 1963), pp. 14-15
25.
The Competition Program is found in abbreviated form in New York City Housing and Development Administration, *Record of Submissions and Awards Competition for Middle-Income Housing at Brighton Beach, Brooklyn* (New York, 1968).
26.
Notice and contemporary criticism of the winning schemes were published in "Seaside Contest," *Architectural Forum* 127 (December, 1967), pp. 82-83; "Development On A Brooklyn Beach," *Progressive Architecture* 39 (May, 1968), pp. 62, 64. Also see Robert A. M. Stern, *New Directions in American Architecture* (New York; 1969), pp. 8-10; Stanislaus von Moos, *Venturi, Rauch, and Scott-Brown Buildings and Projects* (New York; 1987), pp. 288-289.
27.
New York City Housing and Development Administration, *Record of Submissions*
28.
The competition program is found in New York State Urban Development Corporation, *Roosevelt Island Housing*

*Competition* (New York, 1974).
29.
Plans and contemporary criticism of selected schemes were published in Deborah Nevins, ed., *The Roosevelt Island Housing Competition* (New York: 1975); Suzanne Stephens, "This Side of Habitat," *Progressive Architecture* 54 (July, 1975), pp. 58-63; Gerald Allen, "Roosevelt Island Competition—Was It Really A Flop?" *Architectural Record* 158 (October, 1975), pp. 111-120.
30.
The competition program is found in: New York State Council on the Arts, *Inner City Infill: A Housing Competition for Harlem* (New York, 1985).

*Installation of PaineWebber exhibition,*
*"Reweaving the Urban Fabric"*
*Exhibition designed by Abigail Sturges*

## Symposium Notes: "The Future of Infill Housing"
*Moderated by Marta Gutman*

### Part I

*Paul Buckhurst:* B.F.H.K. is working with city agencies. I will focus on the issue of vacant land and buildings to "get the scale of the problem" and confront the issue of how to provide infill housing in this city.

The area in the study comprises 190 square blocks and 1 1/2 square miles.

Via our land use analysis, we discovered 9900 buildings in the area, 22% of which are vacant. In addition, there are 75 to 80 acres of vacant land designated for residential use, in 221 separate vacant parcels, of varied size.

Estimating, we can accommodate 7000 new units in existing vacant buildings in East Harlem. On vacant land, assuming an average of four stories (to retain the current architectural character in East Harlem) and units per building, another 4500 units could be provided. So, in conservative terms, on existing vacant land and in existing vacant buildings, one could add 11,500 units without stretching the case. That would mean a 27% increase in housing stock in East Harlem. 11,000 units seem to represent a marvellous opportunity, and one might say, "Let's get on with it." I can think of 25 reasons why this could be very difficult . . . here are half a dozen of them:

1. Coordinating separate small parcels of development opportunities into something that could attract private assessment.

2. Mixed ownership. Different city agency — owned land and privately owned.

3. Mix of vacant buildings and vacant land with different goals or different ownership in mind.

4. Lack of control (for private developers), creating market uncertainty.

5. Cost. Two years ago, the average cost of renovating small units in either brownstone or tenements was estimated at between $75-80,000 per unit; ie a subsidy of $50,000 per unit would be necessary to make those homes affordable to the average family currently living in East Harlem.

6. Zoning. Currently difficult, which increases cost to work on a typical small-sized lot in East Harlem.

7. Inter-agency rivalry. Also conflict between local community needs and the perception of those needs by city agencies.

On a less pessimistic note, here are four things we should be thinking about:

1. These are "emerging neighborhoods". There is sufficient activity, particularly

*For the purpose of this discussion, "infill" is defined broadly as a process which can occur at the scale of building, city block or neighborhood and include new construction, rehabilitation, or a combination of both. Several comments refer to the exhibition, "Reweaving the Urban Fabric", which was on display in PaineWebber's gallery, New York City, from March 10th through June 10th, 1988. The symposium was held on May 19th, 1988.*

as you move south to 96th Street, to demonstrate a strengthening housing market.

2. Talk of increased funding (for housing) from such sources as the Battery Park City Authority, ie some transfer of funds from high-income areas to low-income housing may actually be in the works.

3. HPD is making a determined effort to package sites together to encourage development interest.

4. Finally, not a given yet, but a need, for increased interagency cooperation which, to date, has been one of the largest stumbling blocks.

*Ghislaine Hermanuz:* Infill housing is not a choice but a necessity for many neighborhoods in the New York City area where small parcels of vacant land are no longer the exception, but the rule. Many architects will remember designing "Vestpocket" parks twenty years ago. Where there were only occasional vacant sites in a block, designers saw a chance to create a small open space. Now, this approach is no longer a valid answer in neighborhoods where 25%, and sometimes 50%, of the land is vacant and housing is scarce. So infill housing is our new opportunity to resolve the housing crisis, not just quantitively, but qualitatively. How can we make neighborhoods better through infill housing and how do people in communities affected by blight perceive the potential of infill housing to improve their environment?

1. First, infill can help create a scale of development which allows for community sponsorship of small scale projects. The City has been interested in larger sites, such as those of Urban Renewal areas, because they attract proposals from developers and contractors with considerable means and experience. Community groups, however, have been left out of this process, because they cannot compete, yet they are very much interested in trying to recreate avenues for local sponsorshop. Small infill sites offer them this chance to build at a scale that is manageable and with space programs reflective of local needs.

2. Second, infill can help resolve the issue of housing affordability by fostering new types of tenure — from community land trusts, to mutual housing associations — which will not only make housing affordable but keep it so over the years. New ways of developing home ownership for current residents, so as not to displace them, can also result from infill housing construction. Infill should also suggest technologies which will make construction at a small scale possible and affordable.

3. Infill developments must also contribute to the qualitative transformation of the neighborhood. It is important that infill developments do not only bring new housing to a neighborhood, but bring along support services as well. Architects must design such services at a scale appropriate to the neighborhood, that is integrated with residential spaces. These services should address present social needs, in response to recent societal changes.

4. Finally — and possibly most importantly — infill housing is really a way of challenging our acceptance of rehabilitation as the fastest way of providing housing to people in need and, thus, the panacea to the housing crisis. Too often, rehabilitation becomes the way to perpetuate the use of obsolete building types

—Old-Law tenements, New-Law tenements, etc.—which never were and continue not to be suitable for the kind of living situations characteristic of low-income neighborhoods.

So, we can begin to draw up a list of strategies to consider in order to make an impact on a neighborhood livability with the design of infill housing.

The first strategy should be geared at *increasing opportunities for community sponsorship*. In areas such as Harlem, where vacant land and vacant buildings are mostly city-owned, new developments have been limited to responses to "Request for Proposals" presented by the City. These requests usually involve sites for rehabilitation that have been too large for small groups to consider becoming the sponsors of such redevelopments. As the City runs out of large-scale sites, which are easier for a "for-profit" developer, there might be room to revamp the notion of involving the community in local development projects.

*Achieving affordability* is a difficult goal to meet, because the cost of housing cannot be lowered by merely adopting cheaper construction methods. Of necessity, to produce affordable housing some forms of subsidies will be involved, and current average levels of subsidies will not be sufficient to make housing affordable to people of the lowest income levels (those who earn less than $10,000 a year). But there are ways other than lowering housing costs and quality which should be explored, because they can help make housing affordable in the long run. An apartment doesn't just have to be a residential space; it can be a place where people work, where they can develop many kinds of economic activities. Housing can be an income generator.

The introduction of *support services* to neighborhoods is also crucial. Household composition has changed tremendously. There are no longer the very large families that, we assume, made up the population of poor neighborhoods. They have been replaced by smaller, single-parent families, or very young or very old people, who do not have speicific or permanent means of support. Not only is there a need for a new housing typology to suit these people, but there is also a need for a battery of support services to address their social needs. There is also a need to create support for these people who might otherwise be displaced by changes in the neighborhood.

*Changing our attitude toward rehabilitation is also critical*. There has been a tremendous push to invest public funds into rehabilitation over the past few years, and that effort may have actually "petrified" bad units for another building life cycle. Turn of the century tenements had often not been built to stay, but to make a quick profit on minimally-acceptable shelter. Is rehabilitation the best way of making new units available to people? In cases where infill is adjacent to sound, rehabilitable buildings, it opens the opportunity to re-think and transform the existing units, improving them to today's space standards.

Infill housing lends itself to more creative ways of making housing affordable to people who need it than the present housing development approaches which are supported by city agencies' policies. On the Lower East Side, for instance, community organizations have organized themselves into a Community Land Trust. It is a successful attempt, at the community level, to establish control over

*Participants*
*Paul Buckhurst:* Principal at Buckhurst, Fish, Hutton and Katz (B.F.H.K.) and professor in Urban Planning at Columbia.
*Ghislaine Hermanuz:* Director of The City College Architectural Center, and professor at City College
*Tony Schuman:* Professor at New Jersey Institute of Technology:
*Richard Plunz:* Professor at The Graduate School of Architecture, Planning and Preservation at Columbia University.

the development of a number of small infill and rehabilitation sites. Not only will the Trust make possible a better redevelopment process, but it will work toward creating housing which will remain affordable. Housing which is affordable only for a limited time is not the answer to the housing crisis.

Community Design Centers are more and more involved in helping community groups to reclaim their own neighborhoods. Infill housing has become a very important issue to them. C.D.C's are interested not only because infill is a means of helping people regain control of their environment, but because the qualitive transformation of poor neighborhoods can be accomplished this way. Because of the social and architectural impact it might have, we (CCAC) have begun a number of projects which will hopefully provide guidelines for community groups to get more involved in infill development.

*Tony Schuman:* I assume, or hope, that most of you have seen the exhibit downstairs. I went through it this afternoon, too quickly perhaps, but I had two very immediate responses, which are the responses I always have when I think about, talk about, or look at comparative examples of affordable housing in the United States and Western Europe or Canada. One is, I'm always optimistic to see the incredible range of possible solutions that are proposed here and there and, secondly, I'm filled with anger that so few of them exist as built products in the United States. And I think one of the things that has to strike you in the exhibit is, although there are a number of good examples of built affordable housing from the United States, there is a preponderance of "paper projects," that is drawn proposals and, also, a fair amount of it as rehabilitation. Although I'm very much in favor of re-hab as a strategy, as a viable and necessary approach to housing, I want to focus here on the design of new, affordable infill housing.

It is my feeling that we are dealing with three subjects here. One is housing, two is design and the third is cities. If I can be a little philosophical, with historical hindsight I would say that as a nation, we don't believe in cities, we don't believe in design and we don't believe in public responsibility for social goods and services such as housing. So in that context, it's a miracle that any good affordable housing is designed and built. I'm aware that there are some of the designers here (of built and unbuilt work) and these are heroes of our time. Because in our country, the architects who do this are not the heroes of the profession. It's the opposite of Western Europe.

I would like to make a couple of bold propositions here, some of them not original, but tied to the specific topic at hand and then I have the luxury of dumping it all in Richard's lap to conclude. It has been said by a number of people, among them Dolores Hayden, that the U.S. has transposed the traditional notion of Utopia, which is generally situated in the public realm and the city, and the particular genius of the U.S. has been to transpose this notion into the private realm and the house. We are used to seeing that as exemplified by the suburban house, which is taken by many as the "sine qua non" of good living. This is not a symposium about suburbia, but there are two things that strike me as somewhat alarming. One is the tendency of new, affordable, infill housing to look suburban. And secondly, I would argue that some of the new suburban housing is at higher densities than the new urban housing.

I'm speaking of projects like the Niemiah housing and new public housing on Avenue C and Sixth Street in Manhattan and I don't offer this as criticism of the architects. Those of you who labor in this field know that it's hard to do good work. Why is something like Niemiah, in my view, a problem? What we're being given there in order to make it affordable, is housing that is factory-produced and shipped in boxes. It is a fundamentally anti-urban proposition. If you look at European examples, and also the best of U.S. housing, you will find that in all respects the built fabric of the city creates a public realm that says "housing makes the city." It is the neutral ground of the city and most of the built space in the city.

I'm convinced that if we believed in this we would find a means to subsidize it adequately. That was an alarming number that Paul (Buckhurst) threw out. $50,000 per unit for rehab, in order to make it affordable to households with $20,000 incomes or less. We're talking in the neighborhood of billions of dollars of subsidies needed. There's a failure of commitment of funds. Basically, the proposition is that poor people should be lucky to get any housing.

We have to applaud anything that gets built now, but if we don't also criticize it we're never going to get better here. Right across the street is a wonderful example of how New York built working-class housing earlier in this century, not semi-detached rowhouses without off street parking. Blank ends of buildings on the side streets are totally counter to the notion of building cities. What is even more alarming, is that in the 1920's and 30's, the U.S. was not so far behind Western Europe in new or even in innovative funding programs. I would argue that a lot of our best work was our first work.

For example, amalgamated dwellings on Grand Street, designed by Springstein and Goldhammer in the late 20's or First Houses, the very first public housing in the nation which combined rehab, new construction and was still a successful public housing project; Harlem River Houses, early public housing as well — there's a fairly long list from the 20's and 30's that stands up well to the European examples. These days it's harder to find. There are a couple of good examples built that are in this (PaineWebber) exhibit.

I teach architecture, and courses on housing. If I go to Europe — London, Amsterdam, Rome, Paris, West Berlin — and I have an architect contact and I ask "what is the most interesting work going on?" every time it is going to be public housing. We operate here exactly in the opposite dimension. Here it's always private sector buildings. There is nothing inherent in our country that says it has to be that way. The reason why we had better public housing in the 30's is because it was conceived of as a construction program, and it put people to work, so we funded it adequately. It has not been the case since.

This doesn't mean all is hopeless. It means that there are some good examples — there's been both this exhibit and symposium. The Architectural League has done several interesting exhibits, and competitions, and NYSCA sponsored a Harlem Infill housing competition, the results of which one hopes will someday be built. It's another thing to fund the construction, and if anyone here thinks that design can solve any of these problems without a very substantial public policy change, there's not a prayer.

We are talking about some deep-seated ideas — "we should leave the cities and go to the suburbs." Not all of us believe that. Some of us believe that not everyone has the option to leave the city and not everyone wants to. The question is, what would turn around public opinion? In my view, nothing will turn it around better than a couple of built examples. You have to be able to point to something and it's embarassing to always say that this is from Western Europe. What's needed here are three things. We need more dollars in deep subsidies; we need better design and we need to honor this architecture and fund it adequately so that our finest architects will be interested in doing housing projects.

Finally, we need better policy. We need much more experimentation. There's a great deal to learn from in terms of municipal approaches and private not-for-profits and I guess we should also be pushing to see what the private sector can do. The problem is there is a serious mismatch between what people have to spend on housing and how much it costs to build housing. There are only three ways to deal with that. You can lower the cost of housing, you can raise people's income, (which may ultimately be the finest solution although we're a long ways from that), or you can subsidize the difference. At the moment we have to be working on the first two and imagining new policy on the third.

The only miracle is that the anger hasn't boiled over to more visible forms than it has. The day that we can make an exhibit like this from American cities and fill every one of those panels with U.S. examples — until that day comes, we won't have wonderful cities, because we won't have developed the will to make them wonderful.

*Richard Plunz:* I will speak briefly, as an architect and from a more personal perspective, if I might. It has been twelve years, now, that I have been working on a history of housing in New York City, a quagmire of a topic which I am sure that any of you who may have attempted it knows fully well. I think that the work is finally finished, such as it is. But what I really wanted to say is that the changes which have occurred in those last twelve years, in terms of the production of housing in general, and of social housing in particular, have been enormous. When I started that book, I could not have imagined the transformations which have since taken place in New York City and elsewhere. The final chapter was rewritten at least twice, and now once again to accommodate the latest news, much to the chagrin of the publisher. In 1976, who could have thought that the figures for new units completed in New York City would drop into the 7,000's per year, the lowest level since the Great Depression and World War II? In 1976, the figure was 23,817. Who could have imagined that official estimates of "poverty-level" population would climb from 14.9 percent in 1969 to 20.2 percent in 1979; and then to 23.5 percent in 1987? Of course, for Blacks and Hispanics the rate was much higher — 32 percent and 43 percent respectively. In another vein, who could have imagined that soup kitchens would increase in number from 30 in 1932 to 500 today?

In 1976, the destruction of the "Ring" around Manhattan was well under way in the South Bronx, Central Harlem and Central Brooklyn, for example. But who could have imagined the enormity of the final outcome, especially in relation to the increased affluence in Manhattan, which has accounted for most of the new housing production in New York City? Twenty thousand housing starts in Manhattan in 1985, for example. (As an aside, that boom is over.) Speaking as an architect, who could have imagined that the architectural media could have chosen to largely ignore these momentous changes, instead promoting what has been a very hedonistic phase in the evolution of the architectural profession in this country. When you put all of this together, it comes as no surprise that the most interesting work in this exhibition comes from Europe.

But I wanted to be positive, and I think that it is a minor miracle that the exhibition exists at all. It is a real tribute to good people, especially the architects and others working quietly from within the Arts Council. They had a certain power and they used it well, and there is a lesson to be learned from this, especially for the Left in our profession at this moment, when the issue of forging a new progressive constituency is at hand. In his interesting new book on poverty, called *The Truly Disadvantaged*, William Julius Wilson makes one argument which probably everyone can agree on. He argues that a fundamental necessity for regaining a coherent progressive perspective on our social condition must involve refocusing our energies, rather than simply reacting to the last decade. We must be ready with answers. I think that this admonition applies as much to planners and architects as to anyone else. The exhibition follows this advice. It is an invaluable start, presently in a vacuum, but in time the vacuum will burst. In my mind I both celebrate and dread the coming next wave of radical chic in architecture. We must be ready with substance.

Finally, the whole of the history of housing in New York City is a study in power, a study in complex relationships between people and money and ideology. When I arrive at this revelation I hesitate. Progressives among architects have never done so well in this admixture. Wilson is correct in that this time things must change. I think that the necessary design ideas exist now, generated quietly by the experimentation of the past two decades. But they must be given focus. We see evidence of that potential in the exhibition. As for the question of power, I am not so sure. I found that, in the final analysis, I could only address this issue hesitantly. I am reminded of a favorite passage from William Carlos Williams' *The Flower*, written in 1930. I will share it with you in conclusion.

. . . . . . . She it was put me straight
about the City when I said,

makes me ill to see them run up
a new bridge like that in a few months

and I can't find time even to get
a book written. They have the power,

that's all, she replied. That's what you all
want. If you can't get it, acknowledge

at least what it is. And they're not
going to give it to you. Quite Right.

**Part II**

*Marta Gutman:* We would all love there to be a national housing program within the next two to three years. I don't know if there is anybody who is qualified to predict that, but someone may want to comment on it.

*Bob Bogen:* I can't answer that question, but extremes have more in common with each other than the middle positions. I sometimes wonder if one couldn't turn around the attitude toward public housing which is that if it is provided by the public it ought to have the least funding possible, so that it doesn't compete with the private market. Suppose you take another position, ie that where the public dollar is spent, it should be for top quality and that long term durability and low maintenance are priorities.

*Paul Buckhurst:* Then infill housing as a program, very well responds to that. Simply stated, if we can design within the context of an existing neighborhood, then we are providing qualities which are not normally found in public housing in this country.

*Herbert Oppenheimer:* There is a national report out for a housing act that calls for $3 billion dollars a year, starting immediately, on new housing programs plus the revival of many other existing programs that had been dying for the last 15 years, including public housing. As recently as today, the A.I.A. has said that suddenly, there are new housing bills appearing in the Senate, which have not been there in a decade. Projections of 8 or 9 million homeless by the year 2000 are frightening, and middle class families can no longer afford housing. So there is a consensus from all sorts of places to take action.

*Richard Plunz:* Yes, I think it's time that new housing legislation is in the works. Certainly, after Reagan, whether it's the next four years or after that, is going to see a major new initiative. There has to be. As far as "social housing" goes, I think that the heart of that initiative is going to have to demonstrate a change — a fundamental change — in what I would call ideology, which has to do most fundamentally with the notion which has dominated our "social housing" program since after the New Deal. That is, you don't give away something for nothing, and social housing must be low-cost housing. I think if the country continues — and this is one of the big differences between this country and Europe — along that line, not very much is going to happen of substance. If we accept the fact that good housing has to be built, for good reasons, and it's going to cost money, of course we're going to do infill housing. There's no question. But that ideology, which has been in place since 1937, is still in place today. It's getting a little frayed, maybe, but I think that is at the heart of design issues. I think this country grew very well in the twenties and at that point it was in the private sector that we built very good working class housing, and moderate-income housing, which responds in every way to a tradition which is continuing, or at least which was revived in Europe in the '60s and '70s and '80s. So I'm not so sure that this still doesn't exist in the national character. At least I would hope that it does. A more positive attitude about cities and urbanism will be revived. But I think the infill question is completely tied up with that issue.

*Jack Freeman:* I'm very positive. We at City College looked at the Harlem project* to see how it could work. It's very important that we talk to people who are in the business of building, and financing, housing. One of the issues that always comes up if you're doing community-based development is experience and expertise and getting a product completed. Government is emphasizing community-design processes and it doesn't have much experience with this. It has a really adversarial relationship with people who do that for a living.

*Ted Liebman:* When you design a project, you inevitably go before a community. One has to look very quickly at problems in developments and then move on. Flawed housing can make way for more housing, at all levels and, hopefully, there will then be more housing and better designs so that the City rebuilds itself. But right now, we're suffering from a community involvement beyond the interest of what that community should have. I think that becomes a problem as well.

*Ghislaine Hermanuz:* True, it is important not to stop the effort of rebuilding neighborhoods, but sometimes the price to pay for development that does not meet certain social needs is really too high. The issue of subsidy and mixing income is wonderful, but it never really happens in the way that we imagine it should. For all the luxury housing that is taking place now in poor communities, on the grounds that it is the only way of bringing subsidized moderate to low-income housing, we don't see anything happening in the other way. There is no luxury apartment on the East Side that is opening its empty units to low-income tenants.

*Ted Liebman:* It's difficult to even tell ourselves why the European examples of housing are so exciting and why ours are less so. It has something to do with, not technology or dollars, but with a small country and its understanding of and need to satisfy its people vs. a big country that believes that some people are less equal than others. In 1971, I travelled for a year with my family and lived in eighty housing projects in thirty-six different cities in ten countries. Every country was poorer than my country, and yet everyone's commitment to housing was greater. What I learned is that a poor person in Holland is considered by a rich person in Holland as someone who needs something and a part of their family. There seems to be more of a sense of responsibility. Before an influx of money, we need to develop the capacity to care before even the best programs can be as good as they can be. It's not only architecture that can do it. Only a few years ago, we built Roosevelt Island, which requires a mixed-income use. That will be so forever because it's in the charter. And yet, today we build for the rich and hope that somewhere, someday, we'll build for the poor, which is an additudinal thing that has nothing to do with programs.

*Marta Gutman:* I think the interesting question that was raised during the presentations, was the question of "improvement", and I think Ghislaine's talk, for example, demonstrates ways in which the community can be brought into the design process of housing. Are there any more comments on this question?

*NYSCA's "Inner City Infill Housing" competition program

*William O'Neill:* I'm interested in homesteads, or "sweat-equity" projects, and I'm involved with some people on the Lower East Side who are trying to do this. Participants are running into tremendous resistance concerning site control and getting any legal status from the city. I wondered if you had any particular comments about whether sweat-equity is an appropriate strategy, and if it fits into an equal housing program, why the city has pulled out of these programs when they have encouraged them in the past, and what can be done to revive these efforts?

*Conrad Levenson:* I think the problem with "sweat-equity" is that it is not just a romantic idea, it's a good idea, to get people involved in the creation of their own environment, but because of the extended period of time that is involved, and the personal commitments that are involved, it results in low production. So if you're looking to have an impact on a larger scale, I think it's unrealistic to rely on sweat-equity projects.

*Rex Curry:* I've been lucky to be in an advocacy design and planning office for the last 20 years. Recently, I got together with a bunch of design centers from around the country which are still able to survive this administration. One of the things we came up with was our "successful" projects. And if we're talking about success, not just in production or number of units, all of us realized that the time we spent from the beginning of a project with really low-income users, was two and three years prior to the actual implementation of the project. I think that there's a real lesson there that existed in the very beginning, when the design centers were hot, when Whitney Young blasted the AIA convention in 1968, and that was the importance of participation in design. I think even in New York it's very easy for us to say, the market's there, just build it and people will move in. We're forgetting the most important part about the design process. . .and that's the degree of involvement that we have with the people who will live in the houses. It may start out as low-cost housing, but I think a lot of people with good guidance and good long-term architectural planning can "paycheck" permanence into that housing. The response over the last few years has seen the creation of major neighborhood-based development corporations. A lot of the infrastructure is there and the planning and architecture professions had better start coming in full swing with those neighborhood-based groups, because they are there to put us in touch with the groups that truly need a fairly long-term relationship with our profession.

*Tony Schuman:* I wrote an article once called "The Agony and the Equity". No one wants to criticize self-help, or sweat-equity because we're all moved and encouraged by a group of people, unable to purchase housing that they need and lacking access to political power, saying "we'll provide our own housing." No one is going to say, "no, wait until we change the national ideology. . ." I always draw the distinction between a project basis and a programmatic basis and I think the evidence is that sweat-equity leaves too many questions of financial viability open, in terms of the ability of very poor people to maintain them over the long-term. It takes a great deal of time and the production levels don't represent a structural response to the housing problem. Only Pratt Center and a few others with a tremendous amount of expertise have managed to keep these programs going over the years, so this issue is less debated than it used to be. It is in the context of deep cynicism about the private sector's failure to produce decent housing that we talk about this. Many people in Europe are living very full, rich lives without building their own housing, so I think we exaggerate the importance of that role out of desperation. Sometimes it's a vehicle for other levels of economic development. The most successful housing groups have gone into broader levels of development and in that sense, as a starting point, it's very good. The risks are burn-out and a continued lack of public support for the participants.

*Ghislaine Hermanuz:* For very poor people, sweat-equity is a luxury, not really an option. So that if we look at the kinds of people for whom it would be possible, then we get into the whole issue of gentrification of those neighborhoods and that's another can of worms. In terms of the City, it is obviously not at all in favor of these programs because it changed from a program where an actual grant was made to people going into homesteading into a program where the homesteaders are just given a low-interest loan for the duration of their work. The number of units that have been produced through these programs has diminished over the years to the point that it is almost inconsequential. But sweat-equity should remain an option. . .a possible way for people to control their environment. But it's not the type of program which really is going to make a very big difference.

*Bernard Forte:* We have a problem on a national level. Housing will not be solved until there is a comprehensive plan to solve the other problems. The problem is only partially that there is no housing people can afford. We need to look at this problem holistically, and we need to look at it now.

# Catalogue:
## Selected Infill Housing Projects

### France
Lucien Kroll
Perseigne Rehabilitation, 1978
*Alencon*

After internal protest racked the community during the mid 1970's, Kroll worked with the residents to develop a "counterlandscape" to the rationalism of the original project. A new school, a community center, and market square, were placed in newly designed courtyards surrounded by renovated slab blocks. The incorporation of gable roofs and textured bricks relieve the monotony of the original project.

Edith Gerard
Quai de la Loire Apartment House, 1982-84
*Paris*

This project occupies a full, though small, city block along the Canal St. Martin. The elevations gesture toward the city, especially toward the views along the canal, while the inner court remains a semi-private space.

The higher "L" along the Quai and the rue Dehayin consists mainly of flats which are designed to maximize views along the canal. Duplexes in the lower building face the adjacent park and housing. On the park facade, their larger-scale reading helps express the main entry into the courtyard, off of which the main lobby is located.

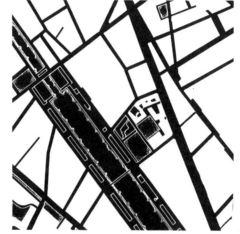

Antoine Grumbach
Quai des Jemmapes Apartment House, 1984-86
*Paris*

This project develops out of the Parisian apartment building tradition. It provides a community center on the first two floors and the basement, housing above, and ateliers, entered off a courtyard at the rear of the building. The apartment house typology, with its malleable forms helps knit together a portion of the street wall at a critical junction along the Canal St. Martin. A brick screen forms the facade's first layer; it peels away at the entry to reveal the second layer which rises to cover the upper floors of the building.

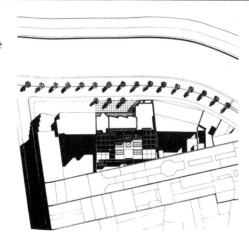

Antoine Grumbach
Mare et Cascades Housing, 1983-85
*Paris*

In this project, new low-income housing, workshops, and a school tie the complex to the existing formal and social context of eastern Paris. The courtyard provides the symbolic center for the complex. Apartment entries off the court, assure movement through the space. The new housing and a renovated yellow eighteenth century farmhouse establish the street wall. The elevations, in red and yellow brick, recall the city's public housing built during the 1920's and 1930's.

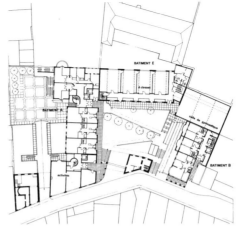
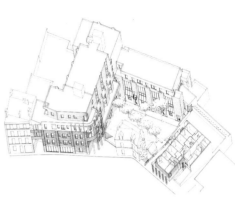

Bernard Reichen and Philippe Robert
Place Fontenelle, 1983
*Paris*

Reichen and Robert preserved and reused historic architectural fragments from Lille's residential buildings as a collage on the Residence Fontenelle's facade. These architectural details, salvaged from demolition sites, bear witness to an existing residential typology in Lille. The quality of the recycled elements would not be possible today, for even if their superb craftsmanship could be duplicated, tight budgets would make their inclusion in such a scheme impossible.

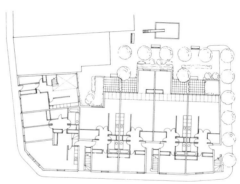

**Germany**
Hinrkit and Inken Baller
Fraenkelufer Urban Renewal, 1985
*Berlin*

This large housing and urban design project reconfigured the Fraenkelufer into a promenade with limited traffic, and complete waterfront residential construction with large yards behind the buildings. It also provided for connections between existing and planned apartments through a center for the disabled and new school buildings.

Curved balconies, cast in a factory, were combined with wood-framed windows which, although seemingly varied, are for the most part repetitive.

Dietrich Bangert, Bernd Jansen,
Stefan Scholz, Axel Schultes
Rauchstrasse Project, 1985
*Berlin*

In this old neighborhood of Berlin, near the Tiergarten, some principles of Le Corbusier's "many little houses with gardens under one roof" can be found. These duplexes open on one level to a terrace garden. The interior court responds to the typology of the old houses in the quarter.

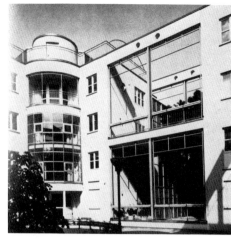

Herman Hertzberger
Lindenstrasse Housing, 1982-86
*Berlin*

The site for this project, is located on one corner of a triangular shopping area, marked by a church. The architect's proposal involved leaving the church standing as a detached, self-contained structure and building a series of residential units clustered around a stair. The majority of the units are entered directly off the street. They also provide passageways into the interior courtyard entry to the inner units. The stairs offer a series of projecting and receding terraces, which engage the street and courtyard.

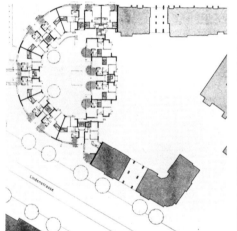

Wilhelm Holzbauer
Luisenstadt Housing, 1986
*Berlin*

What had been a mix of houses and factories was almost entirely wiped out by a slum clearance program, and though a few apartment blocks were constructed recently, this site remained empty.

The Viennese architect designed a block that fills two sides of the triangular perimeter, joining the existing building on the third side and leaving a large courtyard within. The plan creates a mix of apartments, flats and duplexes, each with a garden, terrace, or balcony opening off the living room and facing the green court.

Hans Kammerer and Walter Belz
Kochstrasse Housing, 1985
*Berlin*

The objective of this IBA project was to close the block without making it inaccessible. A pedestrian street links the interior courtyards and opens to the outer street. Offices occupy the lower floors, and apartments are on the upper floors of the buildings.

Nylund, Puttfarken, and Sturzebecher
Self-Build Housing
*Berlin*

This building is an experiment in cooperative "self-building" in the Altbau area of Berlin. The architects provided reinforced concrete frame and slabs and developed a simple timber building system which allowed future occupants to erect partitions, party walls and facades.

Aldo Rossi and Gianni Bioghieri
Wilhelmstrasse Project, 1986
*Berlin*

Like Holzbauer's project, this large residential block, built for the IBA, hugs the perimeter of the site, creating a green interior courtyard for the enjoyment of the inhabitants. It is composed of brick and glass, with green copper roofs and spire-like elevator towers. Its ends are marked by two monumental columns.

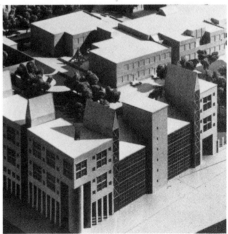

**Alvaro Siza**
Schlesischer Strasse Housing, 1985
*Berlin*

The Portuguese architect Alvaro Siza's five-story apartment house was built in Kreuzberg, a run-down area largely populated by Turkish immigrant workers and artists. Built opposite a preserved row of shops at the subway station, its curved facade accentuates the other corner of the block and maintains the scale of the buildings that adjoin it. The large interior courtyard is the chief focus of the apartments.

**Otto Steidle**
Kopernikerstrasse Housing, 1985
*Berlin*

This alternative to a scheme that was deemed "too institutional" provides five rows of accommodations constructed perpendicular to the street. One involves retention and upgrading of an existing building to the west, the second creates a common space, the third provides new buildings, the fourth is a shared garden and the fifth gives an edge to the garden and closes the gap on the street.

**Herman Hertzberger**
Kassell-Donche Housing Project,
1979-82
*Kassell*

This meandering housing block consists of segments designed by different architects working within differing design concepts. Hertzberger was allocated two separate sites, where uniform, communal suitcases mark the transition from each segment to its neighboring block. Since the staircases serve as playgrounds for children, they have been designed with a maximum of light and air, like glass-roofed streets, which can be overlooked from the apartment. Each dwelling has a spacious balcony large enough for use as an open-air living room.

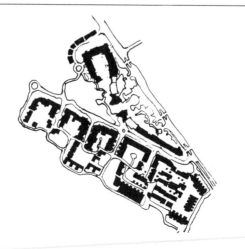 

## Great Britain

Alan Colquhoun and John Miller
Church Crescent, 1981-1984
*London, England*

Church Crescent's semi-detached houses represent a typical London suburban type, here designed for a diverse neighborhood lacking in architectural unity. The facades, (unlike Colquhoun and Miller's more historicized Shrubland Road Project in Hackney) make a strong architectural statement for these units, built as local authority public housing.

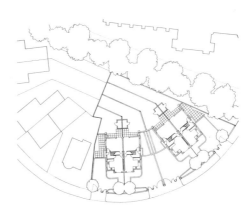 

Alan Colquhoun and John Miller
Hacknay Infill Housing, 1981-1984
*London, England*

Colquhoun and Miller's low-income infill housing on Shrubland Road, designed as a repeatable unit, responds to the massing and facades of nearby semi-detached houses from the 1840s. Their scheme pairs two rowhouses around a large shared porch, separated from the street by a small stoop. The three-story buildings either stand free, surrounded by small side yards, or in attached rows. On the interior, the buildings offer two ground-level apartments topped with two duplex apartments or two three-story walk-ups.

Jeremy Dixon
Cherry Garden Pier, 1982-1983
*London, England*

This competition entry is for a group of sites situated along the south bank of the Thames River just below the Tower Bridge.

A secret water street in "Broom Water," a London suburb, was the inspiration for this scheme. This project introduces areas of water into various sites at Cherry Garden Pier so that the dwellings would have a dual aspect: one facing toward the river and the other toward the street system that is linked back to London.

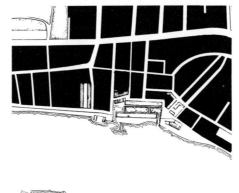 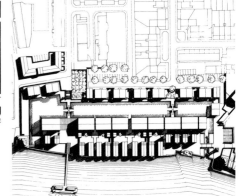

Jeremy Dixon
Dudgeons Wharf, 1983-1988
*London, England*

The scheme consists of a main avenue leading to the river front, a riverside walk, riverside rowhouses, a second asymmetrical minor street, two courtyards, and a small crescent. The concept of this scheme is to reuse elements from earlier infill projects as examples of "type solutions" to domestic architecture. The riverside walk is treated as an intimate, small-scale series of sheltered spaces overlooked one-half a level above it by the riverside gardens of the rowhouses.

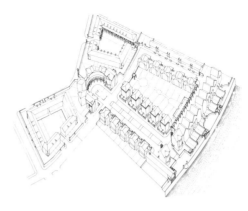

Jeremy Dixon
Ashmill Street Housing, 1984
*London, England*

The Ashmill Street project is a series of dwellings sold to persons on the social housing waiting list. The site is atypical, since it was a narrow strip of land upon which it was quite difficult to build. The starting point for the project was the form of the adjacent rowhouse, which has a white, single-story, rendered base. The base was continued around the site as though it were a white wall from which the dwellings had emerged.

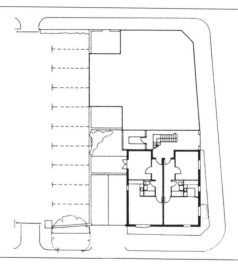

Jeremy Dixon
Lanark Road, 1989
*London, England*

This unusual scheme takes the villa type as its point of departure. The apartments were constructed as an unfinished shell consisting of the basic enclosure, a small bathroom, and a rudimentary kitchen. The purchasers complete the apartments themselves.

The intention of the project was to disguise each group of seven, small apartments as a single, large house. Each apartment was sold for less than half the normal market value for that area. Access to the apartments is between the pairs of houses.

Jeremy Dixon
St. Marks Place, 1975-1979
*London, England*

Each of the twelve housing units on St. Mark's Road, which appear to be a large, single house, in reality contains two narrow houses built over an apartment. The house has access to a garden on the rear, while the apartment is restricted to the street side of the building. At the corner of the site is a small block of apartments. Angling the house plans from the street permits the corner to be turned and privacy between dwellings to be maintained. This results in a contrasting scale between the double-fronted street facades and the individual, stepped form of the rear elevations.

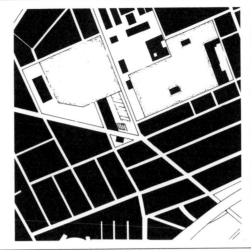

Andrew Pinchin and Peter Kellow
East Quay, 1985
*London, England*

This project includes apartments and houses in tall warehouse — like blocks. The site consists of a courtyard of houses separated from a quayside terrace by a square. The housing blocks are built on a concrete podium that contains a large basement garage.

The buildings recall the nineteenth-century warehouses of the area, but the detailing owes as much to the traditions of the English Arts-and-Crafts Movement as to that of the riverside industrial vernacular.

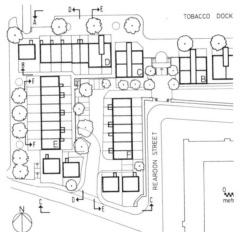

Andrew Pinchin and Peter Kellow
Mollie Davies Court, 1982
*London, England*

The program for Mollie Davies Court insisted on providing a maximum number of small housing units on the site. As housing abuts a busy road, the architects decided to design studio units, with the kitchens and bathrooms oriented toward the street. A tranquil "green square" was created between the new housing and the church buildings onto which the living rooms and bedrooms face. The architects used the decorative effect of patterned brickwork, inspired by the local Victorian rowhouses, and a variety of window shapes, to break down the project's massiveness.

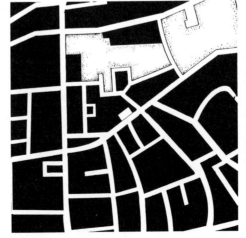

## The Netherlands

Theo Bosch
Niewmarkt Pentagon, 1978
*Amsterdam*

This district had been inhabited by squatters who demonstrated, successfully, against an attempt to turn the neighborhood into a wasteland. Bosch's pentagon of housing forms an irregular, but complete edge, to the courtyard within. The courtyards were originally intended for public recreational use and share passageways interconnecting with the street and canals.

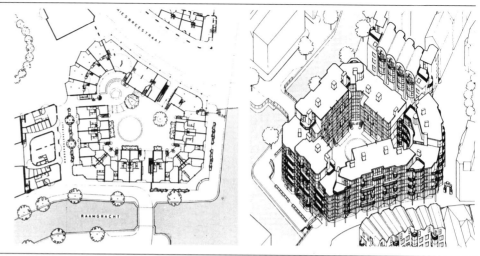

Herman Hertzberger, Van Herk and Nagelkerke
Haarlemmer Houtuinen, 1978-82
*Amsterdam*

The architect recreated a situation reminiscent of the historic city of Amsterdam by closing this "living street" to outside vehicular traffic and narrowing its width to seven meters.

Each dwelling has its own front door with direct access from the street whenever possible. Hertzberger's solution is a variation on this historic theme: the iron exterior steelcases lead to a first-floor landing where the front door of the upper-story dwelling is located. After that, the staircase continues inside the building.

Aldo Van Eyck
Mothers' House, 1974-80
*Amsterdam*

After demolition of a portion of the existing structure, a new, steel-framed, L-shaped building was built, separating the living quarters of mothers and children. Van Eyck placed the children's space in a two-story nursery wing which extends into the private garden. At the street, the new wing rises to five stories and is joined to the old masonry townhouse with a brightly colored stair. Facing the street house are the mothers' living spaces, infant care, and common services.

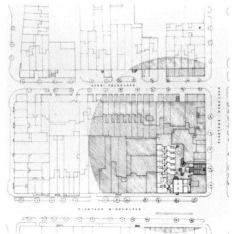

**Architektengroep Mecanoo**
**Caminada Housing, 1984-87**
*Delft*

The plan consists of two small blocks, situated in a late nineteenth-century district, built by a factory-owner to house his workers and their families. For a century this site had been the only place to express feelings of community and faith in this desolate district, aside from the church. The site is surrounded by two-story houses, no gardens or playgrounds, and by narrow, overcrowded streets. A traditional housing type, the court, is reintroduced with modern means. The range of dwelling types is expressed through the plasticity of the facades.

**Architektengroep Mecanoo**
**Kruisplan Housing, 1980-1986**
*Rotterdam*

This project is located on a site within the area that was destroyed by fire after the bombardment during World War II.

The concept for this project, a first-prize winning entry in a Dutch architectural competition, was to create a new housing typology. The post-war housing boom in Holland has created a great number of dwellings, but almost all of them are suited only for family life. In the realized project, a range of inhabitants rent the constructed apartments, including younger people, the elderly, singles and families.

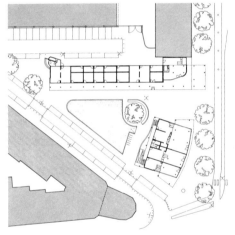 

**Architektengroep Mecanoo**
**Net Oude Western Quarter,**
**(Tiendplein) 1985-1988**
*Rotterdam*

The Tiendplein is a rather special square in the overall rigid pattern of streets in the Het Oude Western quarter. The architects decided that the complexity of the site had to be reflected in the urban design plan. The new square is designed to be isolated from the street which connects the quarter with the rest of the city. Only a gate in one of the blocks connects the small, old square with the bigger, new square. There is also a third, square on a private deck under which cars are parked.

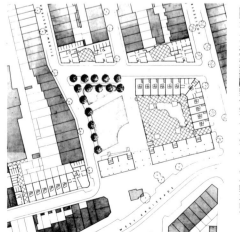 

Architektengrocp Mecanoo
Bospolder-Tussendijken Quarter,
1984-87
*Rotterdam*

Located in an urban renewal district in the nineteenth-century fabric of Rotterdam, these projects consists of four floors of maisonettes. The architects decided that this project should not hesitate to look modern. Because the renewal of nineteenth-century perimeter blocks and the introduction of modern access systems leads to a change in the relation between the street and the inner court area, the new housing was designed according to these new forms of public and private space without ignoring the historic qualities of the quarter.

## United States

Steven Winter, Alex Grinnell and Peter Keyes
Prototypical Infill Housing, 1986
*Asbury Park, New Jersey*

These small prototypical houses in Asbury Park were designed to reflect the existing style, land-use pattern, and density of the neighborhood, while incorporating layouts adapted to contemporary living.

A prime consideration of the project was the potential use of time- and cost-saving factory-production technologies. Bidders could avail themselves of a full range of construction technology options. Each of the houses could be built by erecting four factory-finished modules on a site-built foundation.

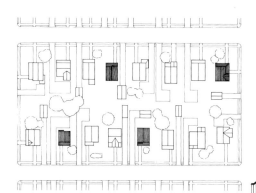

Donlyn Lyndon and Marvin Buchanan
University Avenue Housing
Cooperative, 1982
*Berkeley, California*

The University Avenue Cooperative Homes project provides fifty dwelling units for low- and middle-income families. Made possible through government subsidies, it is conceived as a limited-equity cooperative, the tenants owning shares but unable to profit by speculation. Taking full advantage of the diversity of building types, the scheme has avoided the look of a "project." All structures facing Addison Street were rehabilitated. Commercial space faces University Avenue. Each dwelling unit has a recognizable identity and its own outdoor space.

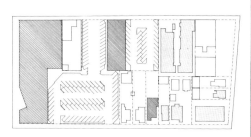

Joan Goody and John Clancy
Harbor Point, 1986-1990
*Boston, Massachusetts*

This project had experienced vacancy rates of close to sixty-five percent prior to proposals to change it to a new community called Harbor Point. Seventeen of the original buildings were destroyed, making room for site improvements and the construction of new low-rise housing. The new plan gives the buildings fronts and backs by orienting them to a street network, and a broad mall providing a vista over Boston Harbor. The positioning of the new housing and the design of the street pattern creates small, semi-public pedestrian courtyards, each serviced by vehicular streets.

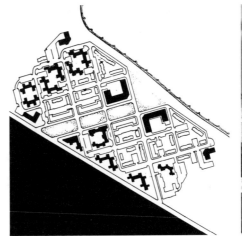 

William Rawn
Andrew Square Rowhouse, 1986
*Boston, Massachusetts*

The Andrew Square Rowhouses were developed as a prototype by the Bricklayers and Laborers Non-Profit Housing Company, Inc., a consortium dedicated to providing union-built, affordable housing. Acting as a nonprofit developer, the union built these low-cost townhouses in 1986 on city land purchased for $1.00. The developer's profit and South Boston's astronomical land costs were deleted from the project costs, making the houses truly a bargain.

Tise, Wilhelm, and Associates, and
Carr-Lynch Associates
Commonwealth Development, 1980
*Boston, Massachusetts*

This project required the destruction of two housing blocks along with renovation of the remaining housing and site improvements. This created space for a new community building, a day-care center, and gardens.

 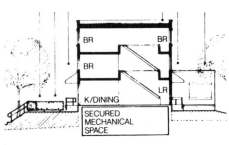

Richard Bradfield and Edgar Gale
Infill Housing, 1985
*Charleston, South Carolina*

This unique, low-density housing project seeks to revitalize deteriorating neighborhoods in Charleston through the use of sympathetically-designed new low- and moderate-income housing.

The architects adapted the 18th-century Charleston "single house." Since it is only a room wide, these buildings provide cross-ventilation in this subtropical climate, while the side porches provide outdoor spaces. The architects captured the character of the historic details with new, inexpensive materials.

Stephen Jacobs
Essex Mill, 1987
*Essex, Massachusetts*

This historic textile mill, which is being restored and converted for residential use, constitutes a major step toward the preservation of the Great Falls/ S.U.M. National Historic District.

Abandoned since 1969, the Essex Mill is being converted as living/working quarters for people in the arts. The eighty-two large, airy units range in size from studios to three-bedroom apartments in a variety of layouts. Most overlook the landscaped courtyard.

John Ciardullo
Mott-Haven Infill, 1975
*The Bronx
New York, New York*

Plaza Borinquen is a low-rise, scattered site, infill housing project in Mott Haven. The planning strategy provided small, private gardens for each family.

This project was unique in its approach at the time of its completion in 1975. While most projects constructed under the Federal 236 Programs were high-rise towers, Plaza Borinquen matched the scale and density of its neighborhood.

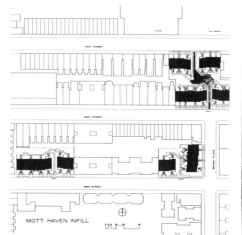

MOTT HAVEN INFILL

John Ciardullo
Red Hook Housing, 1972
*Brooklyn*
*New York, New York*

This low-rise housing project in East New York was built in 1972 as part of the Federal Housing Authority's 236 Program to reinforce and rebuild existing communities. Contained in three-story buildings, sixty-two units were scattered within the existing Red Hook community on three separate sites. The largest units have rooms that are twenty percent larger than the 236 Program's minimum room standards and also have an unusually large number of bedrooms.

Sean Scully, Thoresen and Dimitri Linard
Coney Island Townhouses
*Brooklyn*
*New York, New York*

This series of two-story, attached townhouses is part of an attempt to strengthen and reestablish the vitality of a Coney Island neighborhood through the construction of single-family houses. The 420 units were developed under the 235 Federal Mortgage Subsidy Program for middle-income families. The facades recall the residential idiom of Coney Island. The Mortgage subsidies permitted many tenants to become homeowners for the first time.

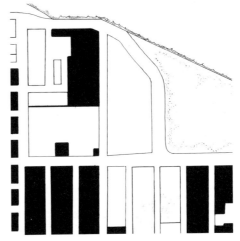

Stephen Jacobs
Place Vendome and Clinton Hill Partnership Homes, 1988
*Manhattan*
*New York, New York*

This project addresses the need to construct new, affordable infill housing within the historic context of Clinton Hill. The street elevations will be surfaced with stucco and color based on historic precedent. Private entries will be from high stoops or doorways tucked under the stoops. Each townhouse will contain two duplex units. These new units can be offered for sale to moderate-income families making less than $48,000 a year, since subsidies of $25,000 per unit will be provided by the state and city.

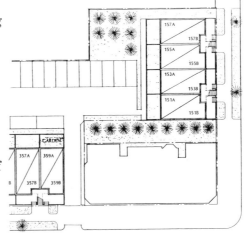

Conrad Levenson
C.H.I.P.S., Samaritan House, 1985
*Manhattan*
*New York, New York*

Samaritan House, the conversion of an existing multiple dwelling into a transitional residence for homeless women and children, is a project of Christian Help in Park Slope. It contains sleeping rooms for ten families, baths and toilets, offices and quarters for the staff of two, a laundry, kitchen, and dining room, recreation room and garden. In order to keep the stresses in close quarters to a minimum, the design provides kitchenettes on all floors to supplement the main facilities and showers in separate rooms to shorten waiting.

Conrad Levenson and Allan Thaler
104th Street Housing Renovation, 1980
*Manhattan*
*New York, New York*

The renovation of this row of abandoned tenements was sponsored by the Manhattan Valley Development Corporation, a non-profit community-based organization devoted to the rehabilitation of structurally sound housing. The architect, faced with rabbit warrens of small rooms linked by long, narrow halls, decided to do away with individual entrances and stair halls, and break through the party walls to create a shared corridor on each floor.

Conrad Levenson
Y.A.R.C., 1984
*Manhattan*
*New York, New York*

This project was built by a community of young people and adults committed to taking responsibility for rebuilding and improving their neighborhood. Through the "sweat equity" process, a gut rehab was completed on an abandoned building. A wide variety of related community service programs were also developed by the teenagers.

Conrad Levenson
The Heights, 1985
*Manhattan*
*New York, New York*

The Heights, a five-story abandoned building in Washington Heights, has been renovated to provide fifty-five units for homeless adults. It is the first newly designed single-room-occupancy (SRO) project in New York City.

The Heights is designed to provide optional dining services for occupants in the first-floor restaurant. Common meals, a linen service, and front-desk management will be operated primarily by tenants involved in job-training and educational activities. A five-bed emergency shelter is planned for the basement.

Theodore Liebman and Alan Melting
Edison Court, 1987
*Manhattan*
*New York, New York*

Edison Court on Manhattan's Upper West Side, is planned to contain thirty-five apartments, constructed within middle-income rental limits. Air rights purchased inexpensively from an adjacent community facility allowed the existing floor area to be doubled. The additional space is accommodated in seven floors of new construction.

The core of the project, a former Consolidated Edison generating plant with a handsome Beaux-Arts facade, became the starting point of the design.

Elliott Rosenblum and Jim Harb
Manhattan Valley, 1988
*Manhattan*
*New York, New York*

Manhattan Valley is a HUD-designated Neighborhood Strategy Area on New York's Upper West Side.

The sponsor/developer of this seventy-six-unit moderate-income condominium is a locally based not-for-profit development corporation, which sought to encourage community development and preserve the economic and ethnic diversity of the neighborhood. The design of the project creates new housing that reflects the New York rowhouse tradition within stringent economic restraints.

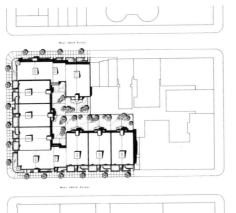

Peter Calthorpe
Sacramento Housing, 1979
*Sacramento, California*

Sommerset Parkside, a 106-unit project is part of a development plan for Sacramento which has as its explicit goals the creation of a mixed-use community with an emphasis on energy conservation and the pedestrian.

The massing offers three scales to the city: a three and one-half story building relating to the denser development to the north, a two-story townhouse "mews" reconstituting the traditional alley, and a row of detached apartment buildings reflecting the Victorian houses on the south side.

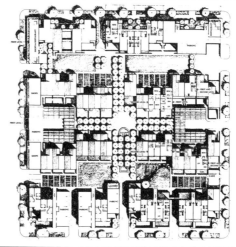

Hank Koning and Julie Eizenberg
Ocean Park 12 at Fifth Street, 1987
*Santa Monica, California*

Ocean Park 12 is the twelve-unit, rental component of a city-sponsored, affordable housing program for infill sites in the Ocean Park neighborhood of Santa Monica. Each of the sites selected had to accommodate six housing units of varying plan types.

A generous, second-level deck flanked by two simple volumes provides the most compelling configuration for accommodating six apartments on the small corner lot. A large amount of outdoor space was created without sacrificing above-grade-parking.

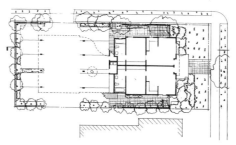

Hank Koning and Julie Eizenberg
Ocean Park 12 at Sixth Street, 1987
*Santa Monica, California*

The Sixth Street apartments are located in a pair of two simple buildings. The house on the front contains two-bedroom and one-bedroom units. Each unit is cross-ventilated, has views of the ocean and private balconies. The "curved roof house" at the rear contains one three-bedroom and one four-bedroom townhouse.

The two buildings are sited on either side of a communal courtyard. The courtyard was intended to be a safe place for children to play and to provide a sense of security and community to the tenants.

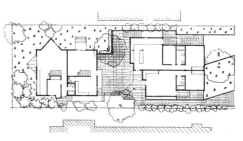

*With infill building, new construction fits into available space — be that a single lot or an entire block — in the existing city. It often uses historically evolved low-rise, high density housing types such as the row house and the perimeter block. Greeting rather than confronting the fabric, these buildings re-establish the physical continuity of the city as they tie new construction to the city's past. This establishes a visual dialogue that comments vividly on the relationship of old and new buildings while it preserves the city as the physical emblem of human memory.*

*Marta Gutman*

## Bibliography

*Articles*

Abercrombie, Stanley. "New York Housing Breaks the Mold." *Architecture Plus* 1 (November 1973): 63-75.

Ackerman, Frederick L. "The Phelps-Stokes Fund Tenement House Competition." *Journal of the American Institute of Architects.* 10 (March 1922): 76-82.

Adam, Robert. "Radiance of the Past: Revitalism in Context." *The Architects Journal* 178 (November 1983): 60-94.

Allen, Gerald. "Roosevelt Island Competition – Was it Really A Flop?" *Architectural Record* 158 (October 1975): 111-120.

"Architectural Competition for the Remodeling of a New York City Tenement Block." *Journal of the American Institute of Architects* 8 (May 1920): 198-199.

*The Architectural Review* 10 (1903); 171 (March 1982).

"Awards Announced in Tenement Plan Competition." *Real Estate Record and Builders' Guide* 109 (11 February 1922): 182.

Bangert, D., B. Jansen, A. St. Scholz, and R. Schultes. "Un Immeuble-Villas: Logements sur la Rauchstrasse, Berlin." *Architecture d'aujord'hui* 234 (September 1984): 53-55.

Blake, Peter. "Riverbend Houses." *Architectural Forum* 131 (July/August 1969): 45-55.

Bloor, Alfred J. "Suggestions for a Better Method of Building Tenant-Houses in New York." *American Architect and Building News* 9 (12 February 1881): 75.

Boles, Daralice. "P/A Inquiry: Affordable Housing." *Progressive Architecture* 68 (February 1987): 86-91.

Buchanan, Peter. "Kassel Lesson." *The Architectural Review* 178 (October 1985): 43-45.

Buchanan, Peter. "The Mothers' House." *The Architectural Review* 172 (March 1982): 25-33.

"Building on Tradition." *The Architectural Review* 178 (October 1985): 40-43.

"Building Up: Council Houses." *Lotus* 37 (January 1983): 61-66.

Camerio, Mary. "Community Design Today." *Space and Society* 8 (September/December 1985): 94-105.

"The Charity Organization Society's Tenement House Competition," *American Architect and Building News* 67 (10 March 1900): 77-79.

Costa, Alexandre Alves. "Opporto: The S.A.A.L. Experience." *Lotus* 18 (March 1978): 64-103.

Crosbie, Michael J. "Gentle Infill in a Genteel City." *Architecture* 74 (July 1985): 44-48.

Cruickshank, Dan. "Under Starter's Orders." *The Architects Journal* 182 (2 October 1985): 20-23.

"Development on a Brooklyn Beach." *Progressive Architecture* 39 (May 1968): 62,64.

di Mambro, Antonio. "Restoration or Liquidation? Two experiments in Public Housing in Boston, Mass." *Space and Society* 33 (March 1986): 9.

Doppelstadtvillen in London-Hackney: Colquhoun and Miller." *Baumeister* 83 (February 1986): 30-31.

Douare, P.,A. Gulgonen, and F. Laisney. "Rehabilitation du grand ensemble Ronseray-Glonniers au Mans." *A.M.C.* 52-53 (June-September 1980): 88-92.

Doubilet, Susan. "1BA '84: Exhibition/Collection" *Progressive Architecture* 63 (January 1982): 197-204.

Doubilet, Susan, and Aldo Van Eyck. "Weaving Chaos into Order." *Progresssive Architecture* 63 (March 1982): 74-79.

"Drawings Exhibited for Low-Cost Housing." *The New York Times* 5 September 1934, p.23.

Eisenman, Peter, "From Golden Lane to Robin Hood Gardens. . ." *Oppositions* 1 (September 1973): 27-56.

Fisher, Thomas and Daralice D. Boles. "P/A Inquiry: Privatizing Public Housing." *Progressive Architecture* 67 (May 1986): 92-93.

Flagg, Ernest. "The Planning of Apartment Houses and Tenements." *Architectural Review* 10 (1903): 85-90.

Flagg, Ernest. "The Tenement-House Evil and its Cure." *Scribner's Magazine* 16 (July 1894): 108-117.

Frampton, Kenneth. "U.D.C.: Low Rise High Density Housing Prototype." *Architecture d'aujourd'hui* 186 (August/September 1976): 15-21.

France, Ivy. "Hubertusvereniging: A Transition Point for Single Parents." *Women and Environments* 7 (Winter 1985): 20-22.

Gangneux, Marie Christine. "Derriere le mirroir." *Architecture d'aujourd'hui* 186 (August/September) 1976: 1-14.

"Garden Space Stressed in Low Cost Housing Design." *Real Estate Record and Builders' Guide* 131. (3 June 1933).

Grinberg, Donald I. "Modernist Housing and Its Critics: The Dutch Contributions," *Harvard Architecture Review* 1 (Spring 1980): 148-150.

Grumbach, Antoine. "The Art of Completing a City: Three projects for Paris." *Lotus* 41 (January 1984): 96.

Gutman, Marta and Richard Plunz. "The New York Ring." *Eupalino* 1 (1984): 32-47.

Hamer, Hardt-Watherr. "Careful Renewal in Kreuzberg." *Space and Society* 31-32 (September-December 1985): 79-83.

Hamlin, Talbot. "New York Housing: Harlem River Houses and Williamsburg Houses." *Pencil Points* 19 (May, 1938): 281-291.

"Harlem River Houses." *Harvard Architecture Review* 2 (Spring 1981): 48-59.

Hertzberger, Herman. "Houses and Streets Make Each Other." *Space and Society* 23 (September 1983): 20-29.

"The Housing Council Plans." *New York Daily Tribune* 11 June 1896, p 12.

Huet, Bernard. "The City as Dwelling Space: Alternatives to the Charter of Athens." *Lotus* 41 (January 1984): 6-17.

"Improved Homes for Workingmen." *Plumber and Sanitary Engineer* 2 (December 1878): pp 1,32.

Knepper, Margaret, and George Stoney. "Can We Renovate The Slums?" *Henry Street Settlement Studies*. New York: (January, 1939).

Lewis, John. "Manhattan Valley Fights for Life." *The Daily News.* 9 December 1979.

"Low Cost Housing. New York Chapter Competition." *The Octagon. A Journal of the American Institute of Architects* 7 (March 1935): 15-16.

"Low-Income Housing: A Lesson From Amsterdam." *Architectural Record* 173 (January 1985): 134.

"Low Rise, High Density." *Progressive Architecture* 54 (December 1973): 56-63.

"Lumiere, Couleurs, et transparence." *Architecture d'aujourd'hui* 217 (October 1981): 72-79.

Lyndon, Donlyn and Marvin Buchanan. "University Avenue Cooperative, Berkeley." *Space and Society* 22 (June 1983): 24-37.

Marcuse, Peter. "Why Are There Homeless?" *The Nation* 224 (4 April 1986): 426-429.

"Minneapolitans Win Ruberoid Competition." *Progressive Architecture* 34 (September 1963): 65-66.

"Model Apartment Houses." *Architecture and Building* 26 (2 January 1897): 7-10.

"The Model Tenement House Competition." *Architecture* 1 (15 March 1900): 104-105.

"Model Tenement Floors." *Real Estate Record and Builders' Guide* 65 (17 March 1900): 452-455.

Moldenhauer, Heide. "Designing With Tenants." *Space and Society* 31-32 (September-December 1985): 83-86.

"Mott-Haven Infill in the South Bronx." *Architectural Record* 160 (August 1976): 114-116.

Moudon, Anne Vernez. "Platting versus Planning: Housing at the Household Scale." *Landscape* 29 (January 1986): 30-38.

"NAHRO Presents Honor Awards for Excellence." *Journal of Housing* 43 (January/February 1986): 24.

"New Amsterdam School." *The Architectural Review* 178 (January 1985) 14-38.

"New York's Great Movement for Housing Reform." *Review of Reviews* 14 (December 1896): 692-701.

"Nieuwmarkt: A Community Victory." *The Architectural Record* 173 (January 1985): 134-136.

"Notes on an Architectural Competition for the Remodeling of a Tenement Block." *The American Architect* 118 (8 September 1920): 305-314.

"The Paul Laurence Dunbar Apartments, New York City." *Architecture* 59 (January 1929): 5-12.

Pelissier, Alain. "Reperes Contemporaines: Edith Girard: Logements quaie de la Loire." *Techniques et Architecture* 358 (February-March 1985): 132-144.

"Plans for Model Tenements." *The New York Times*. 3 June 1896, p.8.

*Plumber and Sanitary Engineer* (March, 1879): 103-106; (April 1879): 131-132; (May 1879): 158-159; (1 June 1879): 180; (15 June 1879): 212; (1 July 1879): 230.

Plunz, Richard. "Transformation of the Tower in the Park — Project for Taft and Mitchell Houses, New York." *Lotus* 24 (1979): 61-75.

"Prize Designs for a Tenement House." *American Architect and Building News* 5 (22 March 1879): Plate 169.

"Prize Plans Held 'Illogical' Housing." *The New York Times*. 8 September 1934, p.17.

"Prize Tenements." *The New York Times*. 16 March 1879. p.6.

"Renewal Gains From Ruberoid Contest." *Architectural Forum* 119 (September 1963): 7.

"Ruberoid Award Winners Announced." *Architectural Record* 139 (September 1963): 10.

"Ruberoid Competition Gives New York Ideas for Urban Renewal." *Architectural Record* 139 (October 1963): 14-15.

"Seaside Contest." *Architectural Forum* 127 (December 1967): 82-83.

"Selected Housers." *Architectural Forum* 61 (September 1934): 5.

"Selecting N.Y. Housers." *Architectural Forum* 60 (May 1934): 27.

Siza, Alvaro. "The Proletarian 'Island' as a Basic Element of Urban Tissue." *Lotus* 13 (December 1976): 80-93.

Snyder, Sarah. "The 'Mutt and Jeff' of Boston Housing." *The Boston Globe*. 3 July 1986, p.17.

Stephens, Suzanne. "This Side of Habitat." *Progressive Architecture* 54 (July 1975): 58-63.

"The Tenement House Competition. Criticism of the Prize Plans." *The New York Tribune*. 7 March 1879, p.1.

"Tenement House Planning." *Architectural Forum* 36 (April 1922) 157-159.

Thomas, Andrew and Robert D. Kohn, "Is it Advisable to Remodel Slum Tenements?" *Architectural Record* 158 (November 1920): 417-426.

"Trois conceptions nouvelles pour le grand ensemble de Ronseray-Glonnieres." *Techniques et Architecture* 348. (June/July 1983): 96-99.

"25,000 Ruberoid Competition Uses Manhattan Urban Renewal Project." *Architectural Record* 133 (February 1963): 23.

"Union Builds Low-Cost Homes in Boston." *The New York Times*. 28 August 1986, Section C, p.5.

"Weissenhof a Cassel." *Architecture d'aujourd'hui* 215 (June 1981): 73-83.

Wilson, David B. "Bargain Houses — No Speculators Need Apply." *The Boston Globe* 24 November 1985.

Woodbridge, Sally. "Community of Differences." *Progressive Architecture* 65 (July 1984): 74-77.

*Books*

Architects' Renewal Committee in Harlem. *Housing in Central Harlem: The Potential for Rehabilitation and New Vest Pocket Housing*. New York: 1967.

Bratt, Rachel G., C. Hartman, and A. Meyerton, ed. "Public Housing: The Controversy and Contribution." In *Critical Perspectives in Housing*. pp 335, 345. Philadelphia, Pa.: Temple University Press, 1986.

Hermanuz, Ghislaine. The Community Design Workshop, Columbia University, *A Housing Platform For Harlem*. New York: 1985.

"Colquhoun, Alan and John Miller: Public Housing in Hackney London, 1983." *Architectural Design Profile 53: Building and Rational Architecture*. ed. Demetri Porphyrios. London: 1984 pp 85-6.

*Harlem: Slum Clearance Plan Under Title 1 of the Housing Act of 1949*. New York: January 1951.

Huet, Bernard. "Alvaro Siza, architetto 1954-79." in Alvaro Ziza, *Poetic Profession*. Milan: 1986.

Improved Housing Council. *Conditions of Competition for Plans of Apartment Houses*. New York: 1896.

The Institute for Community Economics. *The Community Land Trust Handbook*. Emmaus, Pa.: Rodale Press, 1982.

*Internationale Bauausstellung Berlin: Projetubersicht.*, Berlin: 1987.

Internationale Bauausstellung Berlin. *Step by Step: Careful Urban Renewal in Kreuzberg, Berlin*. Berlin, 1987.

Jacobs, Jane. *Death and Life of Great American Cities*. New York: Random House, 1961.

Kolodny, Robert. *Self Help in the Inner City*. New York: 1973.

Luchinger, Arnulf. *Herman Hertzberger: Buildings and Projects 1959-1986*. The Hague, 1987. pp. 244-257.

Medioli, Alfred. "Housing Form and Rehabilitation in New York City." In *Housing Form and Public Policy in the United States* ed. Richard Plunz. New York: Praeger Scientific, 1980. pp. 134-9.

Museum of Modern Art. *Another Chance for Housing: Low-rise Alternatives — Brownsville, Brooklyn, Fox Hills, Staten Island*. New York: 1973. pp. 13-72.

New York City Housing Authority. *Competition: Scrapbook of Placing Entries:* New York, 1934.

New York State Council on the Arts. *Inner City Infill: A Housing Competition for Harlem*. New York: 1985.

New York State Legislative Committee on Housing and the Reconstruction Commission of the State of New York. *Housing Conditions*. New York State Legislative Document No. 78, 1920.

New York State Urban Development Corporation. *Roosevelt Island Housing Competition*. New York: 1974.

Plunz, Richard. *Habiter New York: la forme instiutionalisee de l'habitat new yorkais, 1850-1950*. Bruxelles: Pierre Mardaga, 1982. (Revised English language edition published by Columbia University Press, 1988).

Rossi, Aldo. *The Architecture of the City*. Cambridge, Ma.: MIT Press, 1982.

The Ruberoid Company. *Fifth Annual Architectural Design Competition. East River Urban Renewal Project*. New York: 1963.

Schur, Robert and Virginia Sherry. *The Neighborhood Housing Movement*. New York: Association of Neighborhood Housing Developers, 1977.

The Tenement House Committee of the Charity Organization Society. *Competition for Plans of Model Tenements*. New York: 1899.

von Moos, Stannislaus, *Venturi, Rauch, and Scott-Brown, Buildings and Projects*. New York: Rizzoli, 1987. pp. 288-289.

# Index

## Photo Credits

Photographs are courtesy of the architect, except as noted

*Acknowledgments*
Frontispiece. Alex S. MacLean

*Ghislaine Hermanuz*
2,6,9. Tony Batten
5,7,8,10. Theodore Liebman

*Marta Gutman*
Frontispiece. Uwe Rau
29. Aerial Photos International
33. Steve Rosenthal
37,43. Martin Charles
54. Uwe Rau
65. Marta Gutman

*Richard Plunz*
Frontispiece. Peter Vanderwarker

*Symposium Notes*
Frontispiece. Dorothy Zeidman

*Selected Catalogue*
(Numbers refer to page numbers;
letters t, m, b refer to top, middle and bottom.)

Frontispiece. Housing Authority
of the City of Charleston.
135m. Uwe Rau
135b. Mary Pepchinski
136t. Mary Pepchinski
136m. Steven Koppelkamm
137t. Mary Pepchinski
137m. Mary Pepchinski
138m. Martin Charles
139m. Jo Reid and John Peck
140t. Kingfisher
140m. Dennis Gilbert
140b. Martin Charles
142t. P.A.C. Rook
142m. P.A.C. Rook
143t. Maartin Laupman
143b. Jane Lidz
144t. Anton Grassi
144m. Steve Rosenthal
145b. Nathaniel Lieberman
146t. Nathaniel Lieberman

# Reweaving the Urban Fabric:
## Approaches to Infill Housing

Essays by
Ghislaine Hermanuz
Marta Gutman
Richard Plunz

Introduction by
Peter Marcuse

New York State Council on the Arts
Princeton Architectural Press